Computer Architecture in Industrial, Biomechanical and Biomedical Engineering

Edited by Lulu Wang and Liandong Yu

Published in London, United Kingdom

IntechOpen

Supporting open minds since 2005

Computer Architecture in Industrial, Biomechanical and Biomedical Engineering
http://dx.doi.org/10.5772/intechopen.78476
Edited by Lulu Wang and Liandong Yu

Contributors
Ravi Pratap Singh, Ravinder Kataria, Sandeep Singhal, Ina Suryani, Mohd Mustafa Al Bakri Abdullah, hazry desa, Samreen Hussain, Sarmad Shams, Saad Jawaid Khan, Azhar Hussain, Kamal Bhattarai, Roger Parker, Lulu Wang, Liandong Yu, Dagmawi Lemma Gobena, Andrew Chalmers, Snjezana Soltic

First published in London, United Kingdom, 2019 by IntechOpen
IntechOpen is the global imprint of INTECHOPEN LIMITED, registered in England and Wales, registration number: 11086078, 7th floor, 10 Lower Thames Street, London, EC3R 6AF, United Kingdom
Printed in Croatia

British Library Cataloguing-in-Publication Data
A catalogue record for this book is available from the British Library

Additional hard and PDF copies can be obtained from orders@intechopen.com

Computer Architecture in Industrial, Biomechanical and Biomedical Engineering
Edited by Lulu Wang and Liandong Yu
p. cm.
Print ISBN 978-1-78984-383-5
Online ISBN 978-1-78984-384-2
eBook (PDF) ISBN 978-1-83968-104-2

For EU product safety concerns:
IN TECH d.o.o., Prolaz Marije Krucifikse Kozulić 3, 51000 Rijeka, Croatia, info@intechopen.com or visit our website at intechopen.com.

Meet the editors

Lulu Wang is currently a Distinguished Professor of Biomedical Engineering with the Shenzhen Technology University. She received the M.E. and Ph.D. degrees from the Auckland University of Technology, New Zealand, in 2009 and 2013, respectively. From 2013 to 2015, she was a Research Fellow with the Institute of Biomedical Technologies, Auckland University of Technology, New Zealand. In June 2015, Dr. Wang became an Associate Professor of biomedical engineering with the Hefei University of Technology. In June 2019, she became a Distinguished Professor of Biomedical Engineering at Shenzhen Technology University. Her research interests include medical devices, electromagnetic sensing and imaging, and computational mechanics. Over the past 5 years, Dr. Wang has authored more than 60 peer-reviewed publications, 2 ASME books, 6 book chapters, and 4 issued patents. Dr. Wang is a member of ASME, IEEE, MRSNZ, AAAS, PSNZ, and IPENZ. She is an active reviewer of numerous journals, books and conferences. She has received multiple National and International Awards from various professional societies and organizations.

Liandong Yu is currently a Full Professor and Dean of the School of Instrument Science and Opto-electronics Engineering at the Hefei University of Technology, China. He received his M.E. and Ph.D. degrees from the Hefei University of Technology. His research interests include precision measuring instruments, nanotechnologies, and computer science. He is the author of over 80 peer-reviewed publications and 40 patents. Professor Yu is a member of several professional societies including CMA, National Technical Committee 487 on Opto-electronic Measurement of Standardization Administration of China, and the China Instrument and Control Society. He has received more than seven International and National grants and awards over the past few years.

Contents

Preface

This book focuses on the concepts, design, development, analysis, and operation of various types of computer architecture for industrial, biomechanical, and biomedical applications. The primary objective of the book is to compile the latest research topics on computer architecture technologies and their applications.

The book comprises a collection of invited manuscripts, written in an easy to understand way and of a manageable length. These timely manuscripts will provide an invaluable resource for initial inquiries about the technology and encapsulate the latest developments and applications with reference sources for further detailed information. The methods described in this book cover a wide range of computer techniques that are widely used in biomechanical and biomedical engineering. The content and format are specifically designed to stimulate further development and application of these technologies by reaching out to the non-specialist across a broad audience.

Contributions to computer technologies will inspire interest in further research and development using these technologies and encourage other potential applications. This will foster the advancement of biomechanical and biomedical applications, ultimately improving healthcare and daily life.

Lulu Wang, Ph.D.,
Distinguished Professor of Biomechanical Engineering,
College of Health Science and Environmental Engineering,
Shenzhen Technology University,
China

Liandong Yu, Ph.D.,
Professor and Dean,
School of Instrument Science and Opto-electronics Engineering,
Hefei University of Technology,
China

Chapter 1

Introductory Chapter: Computer-Aided Diagnosis for Biomedical Applications

Lulu Wang and Liandong Yu

1. Introduction

Cancer is a major public health problem with high morbidity and mortality worldwide [1]. Early detection and diagnosis are crucial for improving the 5-year survival rate [2]. Screening examination plays an essential role in the diagnosis of diseases [3], which produces a large number of images and requires physicians to interpret. However, human interpretation has many limitations, including short-term memory, inaccuracy, distraction, and fatigue. To solve these limitations, computer-aided diagnosis (CAD) has been applied in the biomedical imaging field.

The application of CAD in medicine can be traced back to the 1950s. In 1959, Lusted first introduced the mathematical model of CAD and put forward the model in medicine [4]. They successfully applied this mathematical model to the diagnosis of lung cancer, which became the pioneer of CAD. In 1963, Lodwick et al. applied a computer to analyze digitized chest radiographs [5]. In 1964, Becker et al. developed an automatic method to measure the cardiothoracic ratio in chest radiographs [6]. In 1966, Ledley first proposed the theoretical model of CAD [7]. In 1973, Toriwaki et al. [8] and Roellinger et al. [9] applied the CAD system in chest radiographs for the diagnosis of abnormalities and heart abnormality, respectively. In 1976, Winsberg et al. applied the CAD in mammography for diagnosis of abnormalities [10].

The CAD was further developed in the early 1980s, and the expert system applied in the field of medicine was the most noticeable one. The CAD processing includes medical information collection, quantitative and statistical analysis of medical information, and diagnosis. Popular models included Bayes theorem, maximum likelihood model, and sequential model. In the middle 1980s, researchers focused on the development and evaluation of CAD systems. Artificial neural network (ANN) has developed rapidly since the 1990s. ANN is a mathematical processing method that imitates the working principle of human brain neurons. ANN can play an assistant role in diagnosis due to it has the ability of self-learning, memory, and forecasting the development of events. Compared to the traditional methods (such as probability and statistics method, mathematical model), ANN offered better performance in classification and diagnosis. It can be said that ANN is one of the most advanced artificial intelligence technologies.

CAD studies reached a low ebb during the years after the 1960s until the early 1980s. This is because people hope to realize automatic diagnosis with the help of the computer, which is expected too much. The CAD studies are limited due to the lack of corresponding theoretical algorithms and theoretical analysis. This

IntechOpen

dual dilemma existed until the late 1980s and early 1990s. Thanks to the rapid development of computer, mathematics, and statistics technologies, CAD has been improved qualitatively. In recent years, the CAD system has been rapidly applied in medical imaging and has made gratifying achievements in some developed countries.

2. Basic principles of CAD

Computer-aided diagnosis or computer-aided detection refers to the combination of computer technology with medical image processing technology and other possible physiological and biochemical techniques to assist doctors for clinical decision-making and improve the accuracy of diagnosis. The computer-aided detection focus on the localization task, while the computer-aided diagnosis focuses on characterization task, such as the distinction between benign and malignant tumors, and classification among different tumor types. The computer only needs to annotate the abnormal signs and then carries out conventional image processing

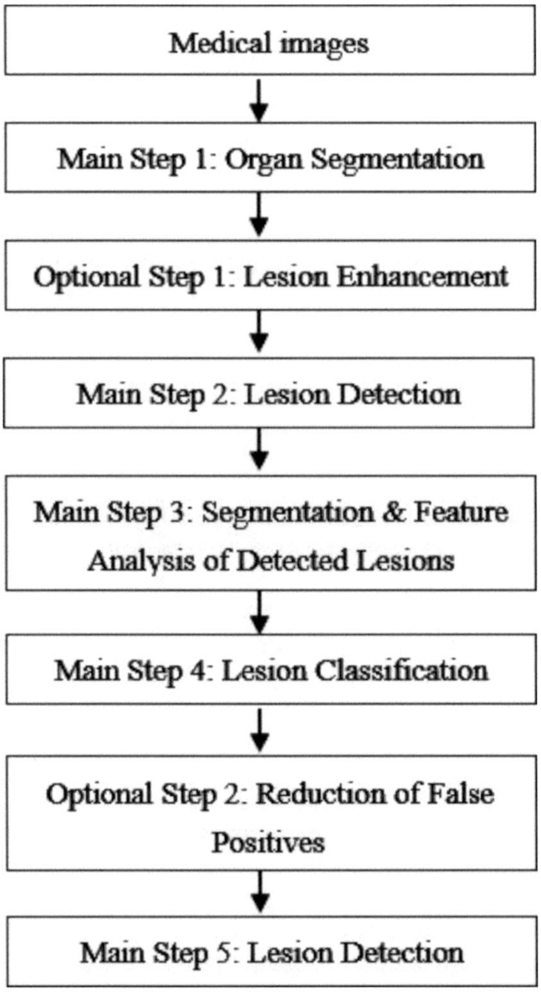

Figure 1.
Flowchart of computer-aided detection [11].

without further diagnosis. In other words, computer-aided diagnosis is the extension and ultimate goal of computer-aided detection. Correspondingly, computer-aided detection is the basis and necessary stage of computer-aided diagnosis. Previous studies proved that CAD plays a significant role in improving the sensitivity, specificity, and accuracy of diagnosis.

Figure 1 shows the flowchart of the use of computer-aided detection in medical images for the diagnosis of lesions. The model consists of four main steps and two optional steps [11]. This first step makes the rest of the steps focus on the organ. The second step obtains a high sensitivity level because the sensitivity lost in this step cannot be recovered in the later steps. The third step aims to segmentation and feature analysis of the detected lesions. The fourth step aims to classify the segmented lesions by extracting pattern features such as gray-level-based features, texture features, and morphologic features. A machine-learning technique has been applied in this step. The machine-learning technique determines "optimal" boundaries for separating classes in the multidimensional feature space [12]. The final step classifies the detected lesions into the lesion and non-lesion groups. This step determines the final performance of the computer-aided detection scheme. The optional step 1 is applied to improve the performance of the system after the first step, which helps to improve the sensitivity and specificity of the detection in the subsequent step. The optional step 2 is usually applied at the end of the system to reduce false-positive rates, which could improve the specificity of the proposed CAD system.

Figure 2 shows the use of computer-aided diagnosis in medical images for diagnosis of lesions. The first step aims to detect lesions automatically or manually. The second step aims to segmentation and feature analysis of the detected lesions. The detected lesions are first segmented, and pattern features are extracted from the segmented lesions. With the extracted features, the lesions are classified into benign or malignant or different lesion types. This system may determine the likelihood of being malignancy or a specific type of lesion.

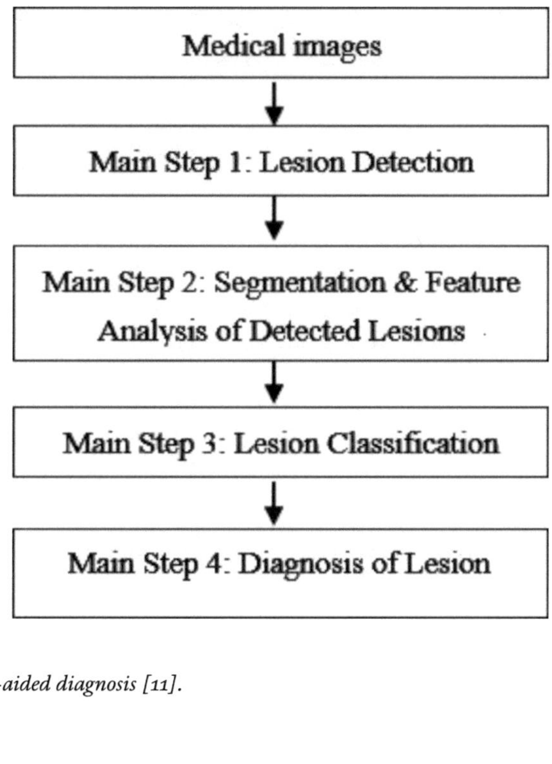

Figure 2.
Flowchart of computer-aided diagnosis [11].

3. Biomedical applications of CAD

Over the past few decades, several CAD systems have been approved by the US Food and Drug Administration to help in imaging situations [13]. Many investigators have studied CAD for diagnosis of various types of diseases, including lung diseases [14, 15], breast cancer [16, 17], stroke [18], liver cancer [19], microcalcifications [20], and artery disease [21].

At present, researchers worldwide have reached a consensus on the meaning of CAD in medical imaging. The final clinical decisions are still determined by doctors rather than machines, but doctors refer to computer output results before they make the final decisions. This makes the diagnosis more objective and accurate. They emphasize that the output of the computer is only a second opinion, which is different from the original concept of automatic computer diagnosis in the 1960s and 1970s.

The applications of CAD in medical imaging can help radiologists to improve diagnostic accuracy and consistency of image and disease interpretation. In other words, the computer outputs can be used as an auxiliary diagnosis but cannot be used as an ultimate diagnosis. The CAD system can help radiologists to improve the diagnostic accuracy because the diagnosis is entirely a subjective judgment process in traditional diagnostic methods, which will be limited and influenced by the experience and knowledge level of the radiologists. Radiologists may miss some minor changes in the diagnosis of disease. Besides, different radiologists may lead to different results due to image reading differences. The objective judgment of computer has excellent advantages in correcting these errors and shortcomings.

Acknowledgements

This work was funded by the National Natural Science Foundation of China (Grant No. 61701159, JZ2017GJQN1131), the Natural Science Foundation of Anhui Province (Grant No. 101413246, JZ2017AKZR0129), the Fundamental Research Funds for the Central Universities (JZ2018HGTB0236), and the Ministry of Education of the People's Republic of China (Grant No. 2160311028).

Conflict of interest

The authors declare no conflict of interest.

Author details

Lulu Wang[1,2]* and Liandong Yu[1]*

1 School of Instrument Science and Opto-electronics Engineering, Hefei University of Technology, China

2 College of Health Science and Environmental Engineering, Shenzhen Technology University, China

*Address all correspondence to: luluwang2015@hfut.edu.cn and liandongyu@hfut.edu.cn

References

[1] Huang X, Xiao R, Pan S, Yang X, Yuan W, Tu Z, et al. Uncovering the roles of long non-coding RNAS in cancer stem cells. Journal of Hematology & Oncology. 2017;**10**(1):62. DOI: 10.1186/s13045-017-0428-9

[2] Mohaghegh P, Rockall AG. Imaging strategy for early ovarian cancer: Characterization of adnexal masses with conventional and advanced imaging techniques. Radiographics. 2012;**32**(6):1751-1773

[3] Sarigoz T, Ertan T, Topuz O, Sevim Y, Cihan Y. Role of digital infrared thermal imaging in the diagnosis of breast mass: A pilot study. Infrared Physics & Technology. 2018;**91**:214-219

[4] Lusted LB. Medical electronics. The New England Journal of Medicine. 1955;**252**:580-585

[5] Lodwick GS, Keats TE, Dorst JP. The coding of Roentgen images for computer analysis as applied to lung cancer. Radiology. 1963;**81**:185-200

[6] Becker HC, Nettleton WJ Jr, Meyers PH, et al. Digital computer determination of a medical diagnostic index directly from chest X-ray images. IEEE Transactions on Biomedical Engineering. 1964;**11**:67-72

[7] Ledley RS, Jacobsen J, Belson M. Bugsys: A programming system for picture processing: Not for debugging. Communications of the ACM. 1966;**9**(2): 79-84

[8] Toriwaki J, Suenaga Y, Negoro T, et al. Pattern recognition of chest X-ray images. Computer Graphics and Image Processing. 1973;**2**:252-271

[9] Roellinger FX Jr, Kahveci AE, Chang JK, et al. Computer analysis of chest radiographs. Computer Graphics and Image Processing. 1973;**2**:232-251

[10] Winsberg F, Elkin M, Macy J Jr, et al. Detection of radiographic abnormalities in mammograms by means of optical scanning and computer analysis. Radiology. 1967;**89**:211-215

[11] Suzuki K. A review of computer-aided diagnosis in thoracic and colonic imaging. Quantitative Imaging in Medicine and Surgery. 2012;**2**(3):163

[12] Duda RO, Hart PE, Stork DG. Pattern Recognition. 2nd ed. Wiley Interscience: Hoboken, NJ; 2001

[13] Dean JC, Ilvento CC. Improved cancer detection using computer-aided detection with diagnostic and screening mammography: Prospective study of 104 cancers. AJR. American Journal of Roentgenology. 2006;**187**:20-28

[14] Suárez-Cuenca J, Tilve A, Ferro G, López R, Quiles J, Souto M. A CAD scheme for early lung cancer detection in chest radiography. Biomedical Engineering: Applications, Basis and Communications. 2017;**29**(05):1750037

[15] Nomura Y, Higaki T, Fujita M, Miki S, Awaya Y, Nakanishi T, et al. Effects of iterative reconstruction algorithms on computer-assisted detection (CAD) software for lung nodules in ultra-low-dose CT for lung cancer screening. Academic Radiology. 2017;**24**(2):124-130

[16] Henriksen EL, Carlsen JF, Vejborg IM, Nielsen MB, Lauridsen CA. The efficacy of using computer-aided detection (CAD) for detection of breast cancer in mammography screening: A systematic review. Acta Radiologica. 2019;**60**(1):13-18

[17] Antropova N, Huynh BQ, Giger ML. A deep feature fusion methodology for breast cancer diagnosis demonstrated on three imaging

modality datasets. Medical Physics. 2017;**44**(10):5162-5171

[18] Bates ER. In left main CAD, PCI with everolimus-eluting stents was noninferior to CABG for death, MI, or stroke at 3 years. Annals of Internal Medicine. 2017;**166**(4):JC21

[19] Kumar SS, Moni RS, Rajeesh J. An automatic computer-aided diagnosis system for liver tumours on computed tomography images. Computers and Electrical Engineering. 2013;**39**(5):1516-1526

[20] Paquerault S, Yarusso LM, Papaioannou J, et al. Radial gradient-based segmentation of mammographic microcalcifications: Observer evaluation and effect on CAD performance. Medical Physics. 2004;**31**(9):2648

[21] King A. Coronary artery disease: Individualize care for multivessel CAD. Nature Reviews Cardiology. 2013;**10**(7):365-365

Chapter 2

Impact of Medical Advancement: Prostheses

Samreen Hussain, Sarmad Shams and Saad Jawaid Khan

Abstract

This chapter shall provide a brief introduction to the prostheses and their development in the current advance technological era. The prosthesis design, control, and architecture completely changed with the change in the amputation level. The transradial amputee stump design, electronics, battery, and circuit placement change significantly with the change of the residual arm of the amputee. This leads to designing the prostheses with the focus of the amputation level and ease of customization. Recent development in the 3D printing and open source prosthetic design leads the user to choose, modify, and print the prostheses with the required sets of functionalities. In this chapter, a brief introduction of the prostheses has been given, starting with the types of prostheses according to the level of amputation and functionality. Then, the state-of-the-art prostheses available commercially and under research will be introduced. Afterward, the 3D printed prostheses are discussed. This chapter will end with the comparison of the medical advancement over the average life of people in general and comparison of the same for countries with low and high per capita income.

Keywords: prostheses, upper limb, lower limb, amputation, myoelectric, 3D printing, state-of-the-art, per capita income

1. Introduction

According to the estimation of the World Health Organization (WHO), 650 million individuals suffer from a disability worldwide. About 80% out of 650 million individuals reside in developing countries [1]. Among 650 million, approximately 3 million suffer from the upper limb amputation and 2.4 million of which live in the developing countries [2]. According to the study conducted in 2016, the population of upper limb amputation is suffering from 16% transhumeral, 12% transradial, 2% forequarter, 3% shoulder disarticulation, 1% elbow disarticulation, 2% wrist disarticulation, 61% transcarpal, and 3% bilateral limb loss [3]. The rehabilitation services to overcome the disability by using prostheses are so uncommon and expensive that only 3% of the amputees in the developing countries have access to them [1].

The prostheses are the artificial devices that improve the quality of life of a disabled person by replacing the missing or lost limb due to congenital disease or trauma or injury [4]. The prostheses may replace the lost or missing limb in terms of appearance, functionality, or both. The prostheses may be classified by the level of amputation and by their functionality (as shown in **Figure 1**) [3, 5–7].

This section will begin with the brief introduction of the types of prostheses due to amputation and functionality. Then, the commercially available prostheses

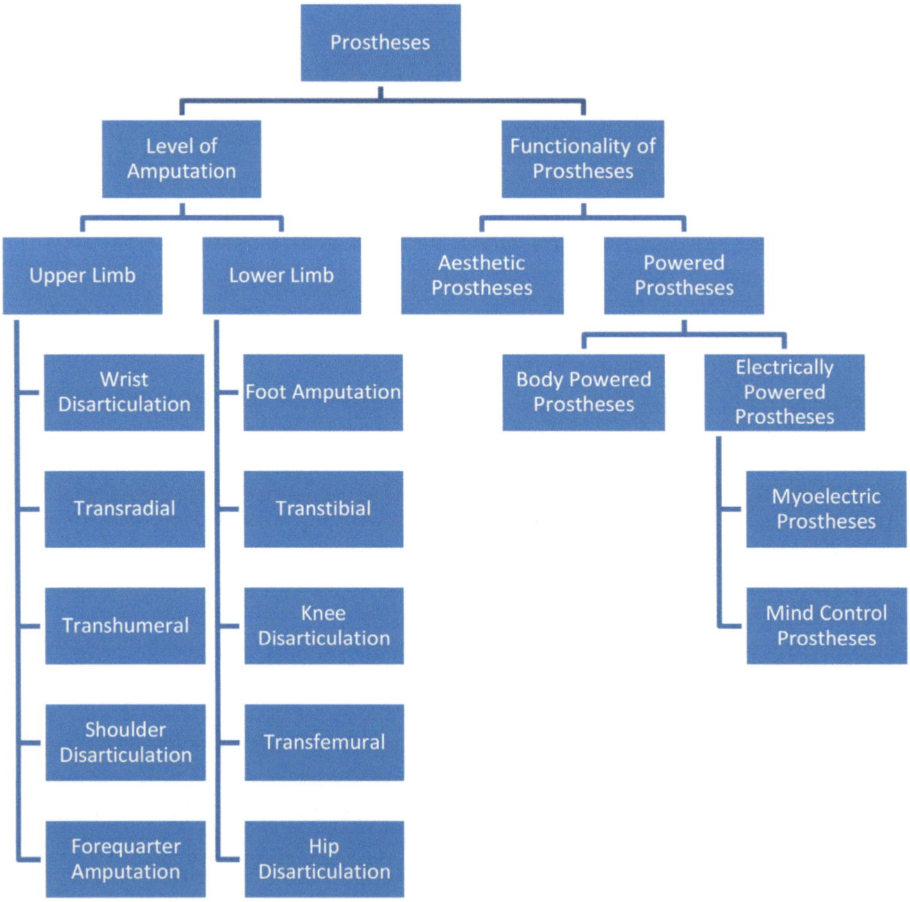

Figure 1.
Classification of prostheses.

are discussed, followed by the state-of-the-art prostheses under development. At the end of this section, 3D printed prostheses are discussed. Finally, the section is concluded with a tabular comparison of all these prostheses highlighting the affordability of the prostheses.

2. Level of amputation

The prosthesis design may change with the change in the amputation level. For example, if a person lost the little finger of the right hand, he/she would only need an esthetic prosthesis. However, if the level of amputation is wrist, then the prosthesis required must have the functionality of all fingers and thumb to grip or hold an object. In this section, the level of amputation for upper and lower limbs is discussed.

2.1 Upper limb prostheses

The upper limb prosthesis design and functionality varies with the level of amputation. There are five main amputation levels for upper limb [3], as shown in **Figure 2**, and each of them is briefly discussed below.

2.1.1 Wrist disarticulation

In wrist disarticulation, the limb is amputated at the level of the wrist without affecting the bones and muscles of the forearm. The amputee is able to perform all the movements of the arm and forearm. Also, the amputee can contract the residual muscles responsible for wrist and finger movements.

2.1.2 Transradial (below elbow)

In transradial amputation, the amputee loses limb anywhere between wrist and elbow. Since the amputee has a portion of forearm, he/she can perform the forearm rotation and also contract the residual muscles responsible for most of the wrist and finger movements.

2.1.3 Transhumeral (above elbow)

In transhumeral amputation, the amputation is between shoulder and elbow. In this type of amputation, the amputee loses all the functionality and muscles of forearm, wrist, and hand. The prosthesis used to assist this amputation must have the elbow, wrist, and hand function in order to enable the amputee to perform activities of daily living (ADL).

2.1.4 Shoulder disarticulation

In shoulder disarticulation, the amputee loses the complete arm with muscles and bones. For this type of amputation, the prosthesis required must have the functionality of complete arm.

2.1.5 Forequarter

In forequarter amputation, the amputee also loses the shoulder blade and collarbone. For this type of amputation, the prosthesis design must have shoulder movements too.

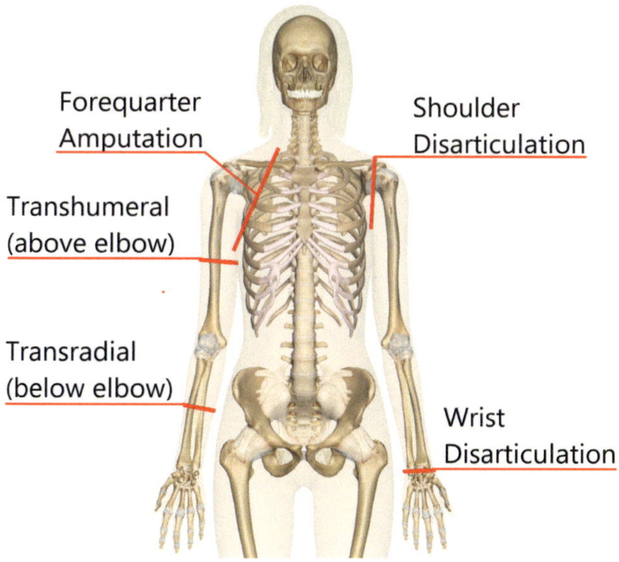

Figure 2.
Level of amputation for upper limb.

2.2 Lower limb prostheses

Similar to the upper limb, lower limb prosthesis design changes with the change in the level of amputation. There are five major levels of amputation at lower limb [8], as shown in **Figure 3**, discussed briefly in this section.

2.2.1 Foot amputation

The foot amputation may occur below the ankle at any part of the foot. In this type of amputation, the amputee only needs a robust esthetic prosthesis to help in walking.

2.2.2 Transtibial (below knee)

In transtibial amputation, the amputee loses limb between the ankle and knee. Most of the time, the residual muscle and bones may be used to drive the prosthesis being used to increase the quality of amputee.

2.2.3 Knee disarticulation

In knee disarticulation, the amputation occurs at the knee joint. In this type of amputation, the amputee loses muscles and bones below knee; however, the muscles responsible for the movements of the leg are intact.

2.2.4 Transfemoral (above knee)

Transfemoral amputation occurs between knee and hip. In this type of amputation, the amputee loses most of the leg muscles and bone. The prosthesis designed for this amputation must include the movements of the knee and ankle.

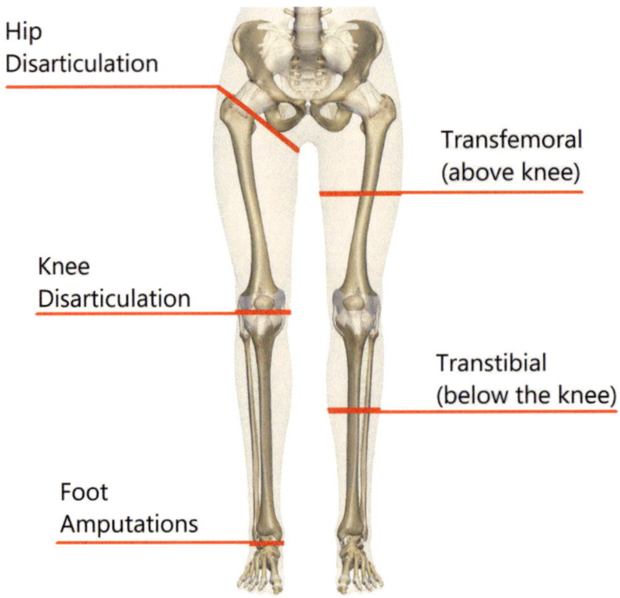

Figure 3.
Level of amputation for lower limb.

2.2.5 Hip disarticulation

In hip disarticulation, the complete leg has been amputated. The amputee may not be able to perform hip movements and may need a fully functional biomimetic leg prosthesis to recover from his/her disability.

3. Esthetic prostheses

Esthetic prostheses aid the disabled person by masking the attention of the public, so that the person may roam around in public without notice. This type of prostheses increases the quality of the subject's personal life by giving them confidence, which is essential for a person to perform the activities of daily living (ADL).

These types of prostheses are passive and have no active component. The main consideration in the design of the cosmetic prostheses is to match the exact skin tone texture, nails, and size of the subject. **Figure 4(a)** shows the finger amputation with a cosmetic prosthesis; after wearing the cosmetic prosthesis, it is quite difficult to notice the amputation of the subject as shown in **Figure 4(b)** [9].

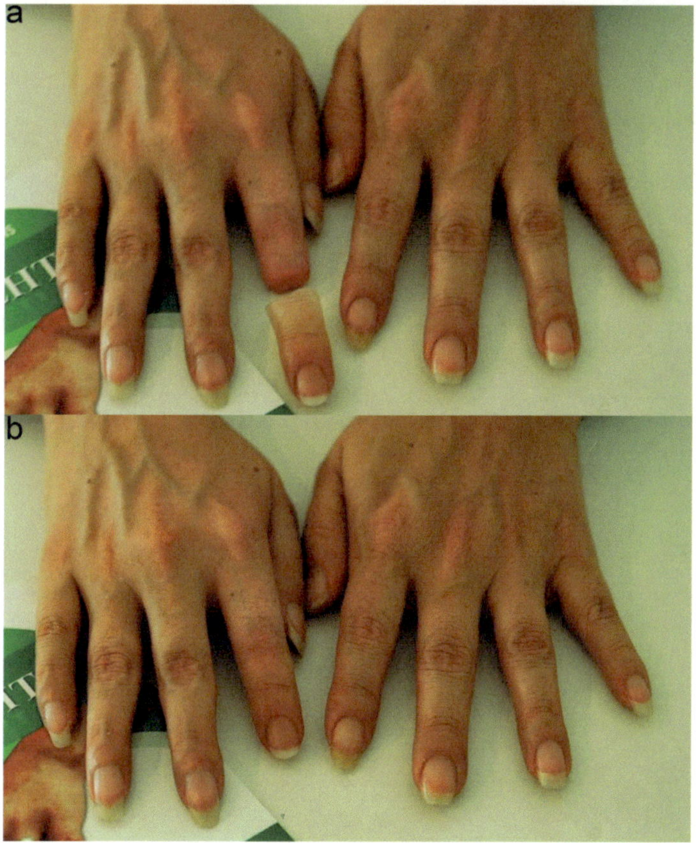

Figure 4.
(a) Amputated finger is shown with the esthetic prosthesis before putting it on and (b) after putting on the esthetic prosthesis.

4. Powered prostheses

The powered prostheses are further divided into the following:

1. Body-powered prostheses

2. Electrically powered prostheses

4.1 Body-powered prostheses

The body-powered prostheses aid the disable person in achieving the functionality lost due to the loss of the limb. The body-powered prostheses also increase the quality of the subject's life by allowing them to perform the activities of daily living (ADL) without the assistance of another human being.

These types of prostheses consist of a tendon or a cable that is attached with the person's body and by pulling that cable, the body-powered prosthesis performs the desired operation [10]. A typical body-powered upper limb prosthesis consists of socket, wrist, control cable, harness, and terminal device as shown in **Figure 5** [11]. The socket is worn on the residual limb, while the harness is worn on the opposite shoulder. To open or close the terminal device, the subject moves his/her shoulder, which results in the movement of harness, which in turn pulls the control cable. Most of the terminal devices in the body-powered prostheses are metal hooks due to the fact that it can withstand high loading and easy to control with a single cable-spring mechanism [12].

4.2 Electrically powered prostheses

Unlike the body-powered prostheses, electrically powered prostheses have actuators to perform the opening and closing of the terminal device. The electrically

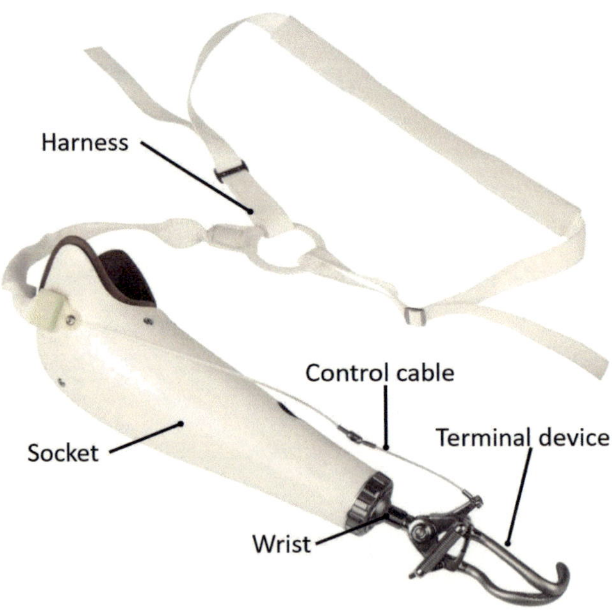

Figure 5.
A typical body-powered upper limb prosthesis.

powered prostheses are more delicate and versatile that enhance or mimic the functionality and appearance of the missing limb of the body.

These types of prostheses usually consist of motors (as an actuator), which is used to drive a mechanism to achieve the movements of the terminal device. These motors receive control signals from the main controller which, after the analysis of the input signal, instructs the motor to achieve desired movements. The electrically powered prostheses are further divided into two types on the bases of the sensing or input signals [6].

4.2.1 Mind-controlled prostheses

The mind-controlled prostheses (also called brain-controlled prostheses) sense the signal from brain, i.e., electroencephalogram (EEG) [13]. The controller extracts the information from the EEG signals after amplification and filtration in the form of features. These features are then used by the pretrained classifier to classify the desired movement of the prostheses.

4.2.2 Myoelectric prostheses

The myoelectric prostheses use the same mechanism as of mind-controlled prostheses. The only difference is the sensing or input signal. In myoelectric prostheses, the signal is sensed from the muscle level instead of the brain. These signals are named as electromyogram (EMG). The EMG signal is usually sensed at the residual muscle of the amputated limb. Therefore, the EMG signals are easy to predict the intentions of the user as compared with the EEG signals. On the other hand, EMG signals are likely to be dissimilar if the position of the sensor is slightly changed or the contraction of the muscle changes [14].

The myoelectric prostheses are the most commonly used prostheses due to onsite EMG signal acquisition and relatively simpler control scheme. The state-of-the-art prostheses [15] for the upper limb will be discussed in this section with the open source 3D printing counter prostheses [16].

4.2.2.1 i-Limb by Touch Bionics, UK

Touch Bionics is one of the top companies in producing prostheses for transradial, wrist disarticulation, and finger amputees. A finger of i-Limb consists of four-bar mechanism driven by a DC motor via worm gears. The latest model i-Limb Quantum weighs 470 g for the ultrasmall model and 630 g for the large model. The four sizes of i-Limb Quantum are shown in **Figure 6** [17].

The new i-Limb Quantum has four different modes of control:

1. Trigger muscle control: this is the default control scheme based on a finite state machine (FSM). The user contracts his/her muscle to control the prosthesis by switching between the states of the FSM.

2. Quick grip app control: the Touch Bionics has introduced a mobile app that can communicate with the i-Limb quantum. This app can be used to control the prostheses and perform the desired operation without sensing the EMG signals from the user's muscle.

3. Intelligent motion gesture control (i-mo): i-mo makes use of the internal sensors to detect the movement of the prostheses and activate a pre-programmed grip on the i-Limb quantum.

4. Grip chips proximity control: this is the unique programmable feature introduced in i-Limb quantum; whenever the user moves his/her hand near the grip chip, the pre-programmed grip will be enabled, allowing the user to quickly use that specific grip.

Although the Touch Bionics has developed a state-of-the-art prosthesis, there is always a room for improvement. Lack of sensory feedback to control the grip limits the performance of the i-Limb. Also, the user must select from the defined grips available with the model and preprogram them. Another factor that limits the amputee to get the i-Limb prostheses is the high price tag [18].

4.2.2.2 Bebionics by Ottobock, Germany

The Ottobock company has a wide variety of prostheses, including both upper limb and lower limb solutions. For consistency, the upper limb hand myoelectric prosthesis of Ottobock, i.e., Bebionics, is discussed in this section.

The Bebionic is available in three sizes and weighs between 390 and 600 g, as shown in **Figure 7** [19]. Each finger of Bebionics is driven by a custom linear actuator through four-bar mechanism. Similar to i-Limb quantum, the Bebionic has an FSM-based control scheme to select among the 14 different grip patterns and hand positions [20].

The structure of the Bebionic is developed using aerospace industry grade aluminum, which gives it a robust structure and is lightweight. The Bebionic suffer from the same constraints as of i-Limb due to unavailability of the sensory feedback, pre-programmed grip pattern, and high cost.

4.2.2.3 Vincent Hand by Vincent Systems GmbH, Germany

The Vincent Systems GmbH is specialized in producing the myoelectric prosthesis hand. Currently, Vincent Evolution 3 has been released with four different sizes, i.e., extra small, small, medium, and large. The extra-small size of Vincent Evolution 3 is the lightest myoelectric prosthesis hand, which weighs only 386 g with the transcarpal wrist [21] (**Figure 8**).

Each finger of Vincent Evolution 3 comprises of a DC motor that drives the four-bar mechanism with the help of worm gear to achieve the flexion-extension of the finger. The control scheme of Vincent Hand is a specialized type of FSM, which senses two EMG signals and can attain five different grip groups directly from the central hand position. Another advantage of the Vincent FSM is that you can jump to the central hand position from any grip by a long "open" signal. The "open," "close," and "trigger" are customizable and the user may choose any other unique signal instead of co-contraction [22].

Similar to Bebionics and i-Limb, Vincent Evolution 3 lacks the sensory feedback essential to control the grip force. Therefore, Vincent Evolution 3 has preprogrammed grips and fingers are coupled with open/close function.

4.2.2.4 Modular prosthetic limb by John Hopkins Applied physics Lab, USA

The modular prosthetic limb (MPL) is the most advanced prosthesis hand developed by the John Hopkins Applied Physics Lab, USA, under the umbrella of Revolutionizing Prosthetics 2009 (RP 2009) [23]. Unlike the commercially available prostheses, MPL contains motor at each joint of the finger. The MPL has 26 degrees of freedom (DOF) including wrist, elbow, and shoulder movements.

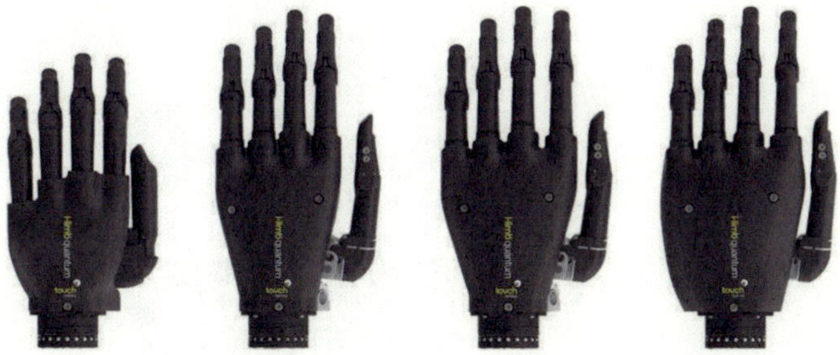

Figure 6.
i-Limb Quantum by Touch Bionics, from left to right: extra small, small, medium, and large.

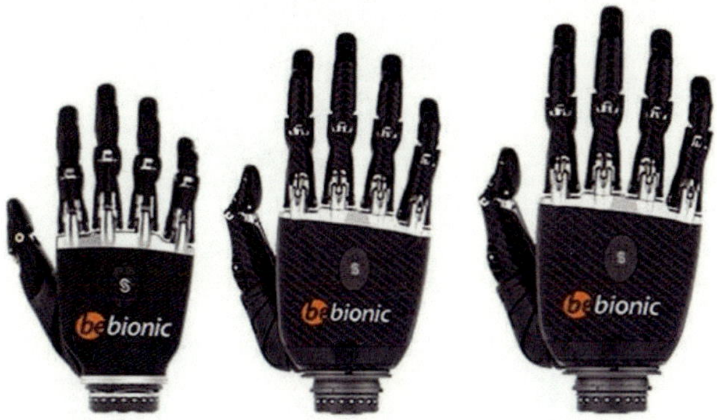

Figure 7.
The Bebionics V3 by Ottobock, from left to right: small, medium, and large.

The MPL is customizable and can be used for all major upper limb amputation. The overall weight of the MPL is 3.5 kg, and the hand with wrist weighs around 1.32 kg as shown in **Figure 9**.

The MPL is tested on human subjects who underwent targeted muscle reinnervation (TMR) surgery [24]. The TMR surgery is the process of connecting the residual motor nerves of lost muscle into the nearest large muscle, so that, the intentions of moving the lost muscle can be detected. This technique is quite useful for a person who lost a major portion of his/her limb.

The recent development in targeted sensory reinnervation (TSR) technique [25] allows the MPL to send the sensory feedback directly to the nerves of the lost limbs. This is the major limitation of the commercial prostheses that MPL has overcome [26]. In TSR surgery, the residual sensory nerves are connected or reinnervate at the nearest large muscle, so that, the sensory feedback of the prostheses can be sensed via the electrode. The MPL is the most advanced prostheses, and it is not commercially available yet.

4.2.2.5 Vanderbilt hand by Vanderbilt University, USA

The researchers at the Center for Intelligent Mechatronics Lab at Vanderbilt University, USA, have developed a 9 DOF prosthesis hand with 4 degrees of control (DOC). The Vanderbilt hand uses four motors with a tendon-spring mechanism to achieve essential grips to perform ADL. Instead of using a single motor for each finger, Vanderbilt hand uses one motor for the index finger, two motors for thumb, and one motor for remaining three fingers (i.e., middle, ring, and pinky). The adult human hand-sized Vanderbilt hand weighs around 546 g as shown in **Figure 10** [27].

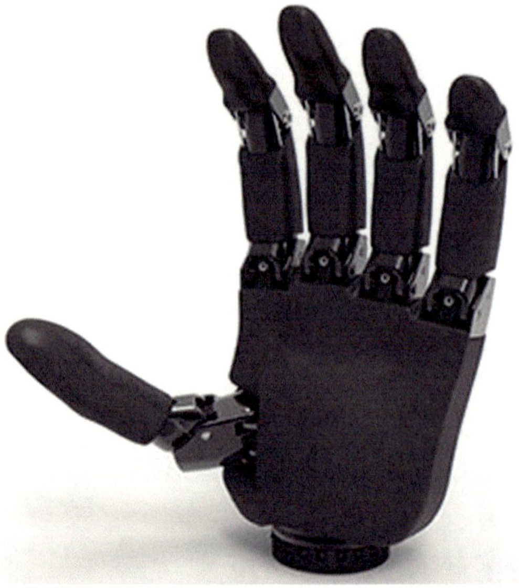

Figure 8.
Vincent evolution 3 by Vincent Systems GmbH.

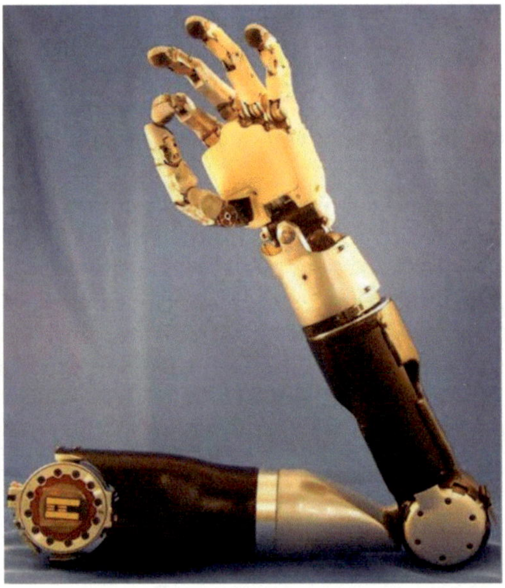

Figure 9.
The modular prosthetic limb by John Hopkins Applied Physics Laboratory, USA.

The FSM of Vanderbilt hands is shown in **Figure 11** [28]. The Vanderbilt hand uses two onsite EMG signals for switching between the states of the machine. The co-contraction will be used for thumb reposition and opposition states. The contraction of the forearm flexor is associated with the upward movement, and contraction of the forearm extensor is associated with the downward movement as shown in the state diagram of the Vanderbilt hand.

The Vanderbilt hand has a unique mechanism and control scheme, but it lacks the functionality and features offered by the MPL. However, the price estimation of the Vanderbilt hand is much lower as compared to the MPL.

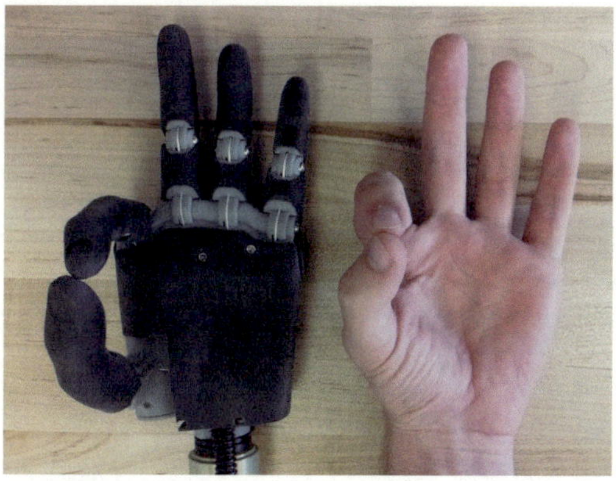

Figure 10.
Third-generation Vanderbilt hand by the Center for Intelligent Mechatronics.

4.2.2.6 Hero Arm by Open Bionics, UK

The Open Bionics has released multiple open source 3D printed prostheses including, Dextrus Hand, Ada Hand, Brunel hand, and Hero Arm. The latest and most advance among all, i.e., the Hero Arm is shown in **Figure 12**. The Hero Arm is designed for a person with transradial amputation. There are two versions of the Hero Arm, one with four-motor-drive mechanism and other with three-motor-drive mechanism. The only difference is that the index and middle fingers are actuated with a single motor in a three-motor version.

The Hero Arm has tendon-flexure-based mechanism for flexion extension of the finger. The control scheme of the Hero Arm consists of FSM that utilizes the contraction of wrist flexion and extension muscles. The trigger signal for switching the grip is open signal, pause, and then holds the open signal for 1 s. Further details of the Hero Arm can be found at [29].

The main advantages of the 3D printed prostheses are low cost, easy modification, and customization. On the other hand, 3D printed prostheses mostly lack the performance and robustness offered by the commercial prostheses [16].

4.2.2.7 Tact Hand by University of Illinois, USA

The Tact Hand is another open source prosthesis hand developed by the researchers at the University of Illinois. Each finger of the Tact Hand is driven by a DC motor through the string. The string is attached with the underactuated four-bar mechanism of the finger. As the motor rotates clockwise, it winds up the string on the spool, creating tension in the string, which in turn flexes the finger. The rubber band attached at the back of the finger assists in the extension of the finger when the motor rotates anticlockwise, releasing the tension in the spring as shown in **Figure 13** [30].

Tact Hand is the cheapest 3D printed prostheses as claimed by the author [30]. However, it lacks the esthetic look, robustness, and durability, offered by most of the commercial prostheses.

Table 1 summarizes the characteristics of the commercial and 3D printed hand prostheses discussed in this section. All the prostheses use an underactuated mechanism to reduce the complexity of the hand design. Underactuated mechanism not only reduces the requirement of the actuators at each joint, but also simplifies the control scheme of the hand, which in turn reduces the weight of the prosthetic

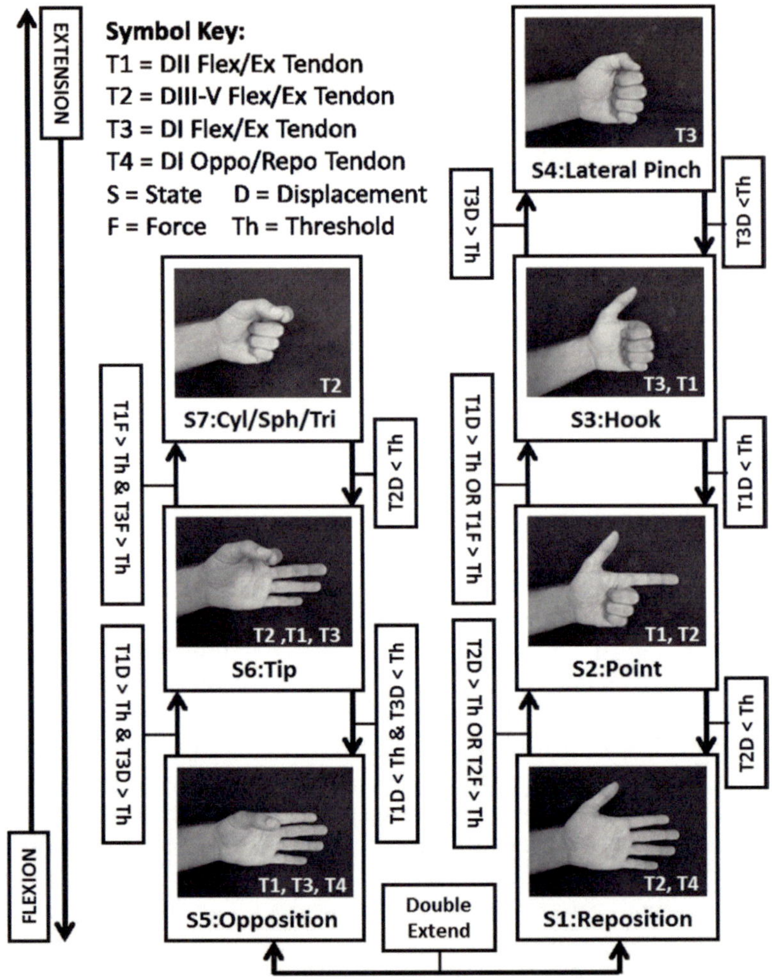

Figure 11.
The finite state machine of the Vanderbilt hands.

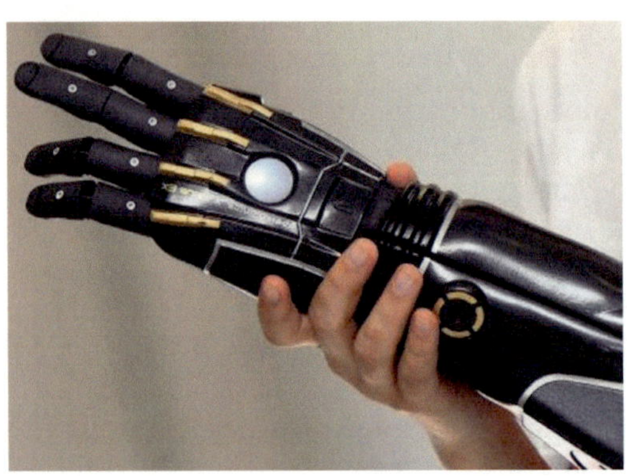

Figure 12.
The Hero Arm from Open Bionics.

hand. The Hero Arm is the lightest among the studied prostheses with weight as low as 280 g. The actuator used by the commercial and 3D printing prostheses is DC motor. The most common configuration is to use DC motor with worm gear, lead screw or spool, and tendon to translate the motor rotation into the finger flexion

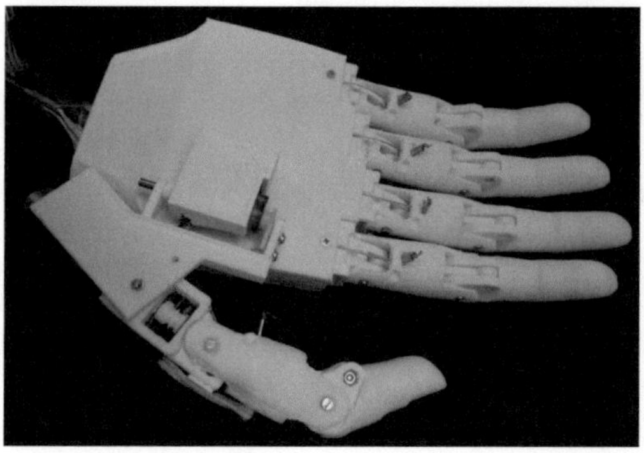

Figure 13.
Tact: an open source hand prosthesis.

Hand/ developer	Mass (g)	Size (L × W × H) (mm)	Joints/ DOF	No. of actuators	Actuation method	Joint coupling	Cost (USD)
Tact/ University of Illinois [30]	350	200 × 98 × 27	11/6	6	DC motor-tendons	Linkage spanning MCP to PIP	250*
Ada V1.1/ Open Bionics [31]	380	215 × 178 × 58	10/5	5	Linear actuator tendons	Tendon linking to MCP to the fingertip	1200
Hero Arm/ Open Bionics [29]	280–346	—	10/3–4	3–4	DC motor tendons	Tendon linking to MCP to the fingertip	—
i-Limb/ Touch Bionics [17]	450–615	180–182 × 75–80 × 35–41	11/6	6	DC motor-worm gear	Tendon linking to MCP to PIP	40,000
Bebionic V2/ RSL Steeper [32]	495–539	190–200 × 84–92 × 50	11/6	5	DC motor-lead screw	Linkage spanning MCP to PIP	35,000
Vincent Hand/ Vincent System [21]	—	—	11/6	6	DC motor-worm gear	Linkage spanning MCP to PIP	—

**Exclusive of motors and circuit cost.*

Table 1.
Characteristic comparison of the prosthesis hand.

extension through the four-bar mechanism. This mechanism is housed inside each finger/thumb with the dimension as close as the dimension of a normal healthy adult for large size prosthesis and relatively smaller for medium and small versions to fit younger subjects.

5. Impact of advancement in prostheses and medical devices

Owing to the technological boom in the twenty-first century, the healthcare industry has also advanced considerably. This progress is evident in all subfields of the healthcare systems. Surgical procedures have moved on from bone drillings to innovations like robotic surgeries, MARVEL (multiangle rear-viewing endoscopic tool), and surgical glasses. The field of biomedical imaging has advanced from x-ray imaging to molecular imaging. Likewise, rehabilitation engineering has moved on from wooden dentures and minimalist crutches to cyborg body prostheses. Pharmaceutics has now headed toward immunotherapy, pharmacogenetic testing, and RNA therapeutics.

It is now a common notion that such rapid advancement in biomedical innovation and research is the leading cause of improvement in the quality of human life and longevity [33]. A number of studies credit this increase in longevity to the pharmaceutical innovations, which has appeared to be the most research-intensive subfield of the healthcare industry. Lichtenberg has proved time and again that pharmaceutical innovations have a profound effect on health and longevity [34–41]. By his research, he cemented the notion that drug innovations decrease mortality rate, hospitalization rate, and improve the general well-being of the society.

Through similar studies, authors have linked the advancement in biomedical innovations to increase the longevity and general betterment of health. For example, Cutler et al. concluded that the ultimate determinant of health is scientific advancement and progress, which in turn is influenced by economic and academic growth [42]. Another study considering the USA population found that the improved health of genial Americans is owing to the advancement in medical technologies [43]. Fuchs also asserts that the primary cause of increased longevity is the fruit of biomedical innovations after the Second World War [44]. Furthermore, the National Institutes of Health (NIH) claims that their research has enabled average Americans to live 30 years more (in 2012) than they did in 1900 [45]. The variables, inspected the most in such studies, are the medical services and procedures prevalent in the population and the availability of drugs and healthcare artifacts for the people. Lichtenberg studied medical care and behavioral risk factors in increasing or decreasing longevity [46].

While the outcome variable that is usually inspected in these studies is longevity, defined as "a long duration of individual life" or "the length of life" by Merriam-Webster Dictionary [47], another important outcome measure is the performance of activities of daily living (ADLs) under the influence of medical interventions.

The effects of biomedical innovations other than pharmaceutical innovations on health and longevity are comparatively more difficult to gauge as there are fewer researches on this topic. As evident from the fact that more than 50% of the research on biomedical innovations is provided by pharmaceutical companies, other researches take a back seat [48].

In most of the cases, the biomedical technological advancements are not easy to gauge. An extensive amount of data is required to measure the availability of healthcare facilities, and even more difficult is to quantify the qualitative nature of the healthcare facilities. In order to solve this problem, a surrogate measure is taken for the biomedical advancement that is the per capita income of the population in consideration. The reliability of gross domestic product (GDP) as an indicator of biomedical advancement is asserted by the World Health Organization (WHO) when it continuously lauds France for its excellent biomedical system, with a GDP per capita of USD 46732 in 2019. Furthermore, the Organization for Economic Co-operation and Development (OECD), in its official magazine, the OECD Observer, reports that a 10% increase in life expectancy makes up an annual 0.3–0.4% growth in the economy, proving that the relationship is bidirectional [49]. On the other hand, the countries with lower GDP have been reported to have a life expectancy rate by a study that analyzed the 213 years' worth of data [50]. One obvious reason for this relationship is the fact that people with less economic stability tend to avoid getting treatment for "minor" health issues such as malaria, flu, and infections. This leads to worsening of the symptoms and eventually casualties that would otherwise have been easily avoided. Also, if there is an endemic in the country like Ebola, tourism and foreign visits tend to dry up, setting back the economy further.

Taking this into consideration, we attempted to find a relationship between the GDP of the countries of the world with the expected life in years for the year 2018. The methodology and results are stated in the following sections.

6. Data acquisition

In order to analyze the annual per capita income of the countries, the World Economic Outlook database of the International Monetary Fund (IMF) was accessed, as provided freely by the Gapminder Foundation [51]. The data from 183 countries for 10 years (2009–2018) were filtered to match the available data of the life expectancy rate of different countries. The estimated lifespans of the countries were retrieved from Geobase [52].

7. Regression analysis

For statistical analysis of the data, we performed regression analysis via IBM SPSS Statistics. The regression analyses are performed taking GDP as the independent variable and life expectancy as the dependent variable. We used the natural logarithm to GDP values. The resultant R^2 values are plotted in **Figure 14**.

It is evident from the graph that over the decade, the GDP alone explains 47–69% of the cross-country variation in life expectancy. This strengthens the notion that GDP per capita income is an important contributor in prolonging the life of the individuals.

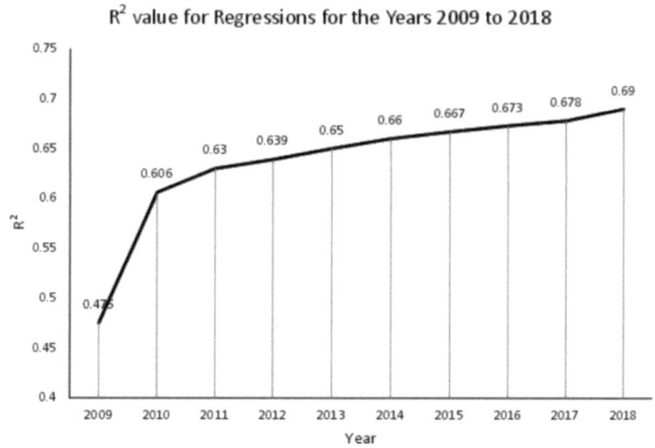

Figure 14.
R^2 values for cross-sectional regressions by years.

8. Quartile mapping

For the sake of ease, we mapped the GDP per capita income and life expectancy for 2018 on the world map, see **Figures 15** and **16**. The mapping is done by first defining four quartiles of each variable. The cutoff points for each quartile are mentioned in the captions of these two figures. By keeping the color coding same for

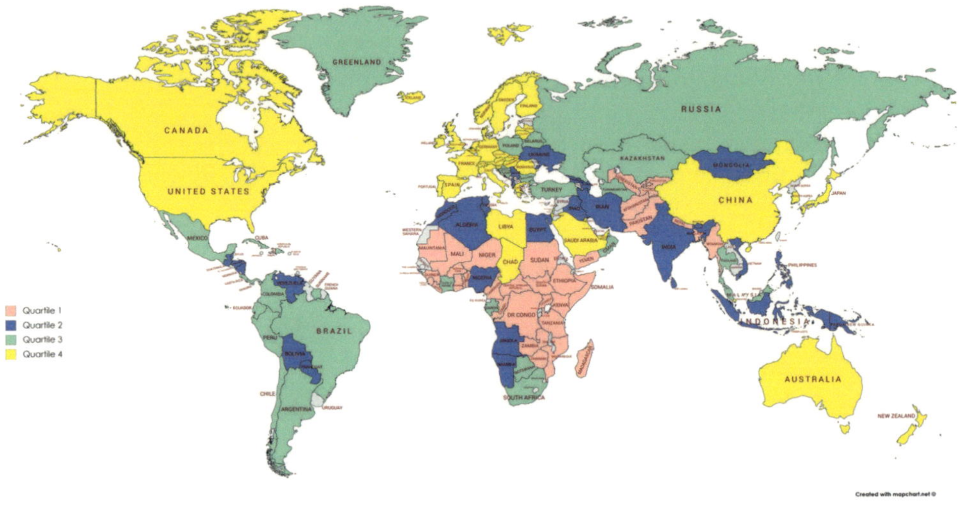

Figure 15.
Mapping of the world according to the four quartiles of the GDP per capita income of the countries. Where quartile 1 is 0 to 2297.5 USD, quartile 2 is 2297.6 to 5874 USD, quartile 3 is 5874.1 to 17617.5 USD, and quartile 4 is 17617.6 to 129,710 USD.

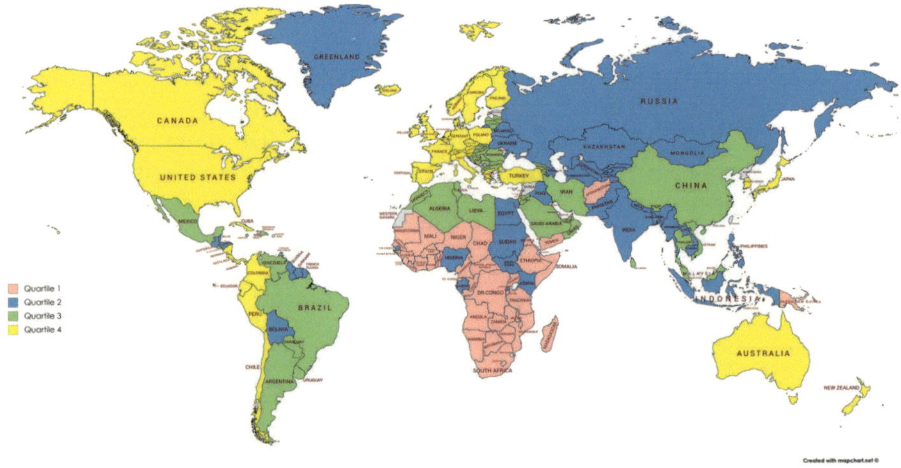

Figure 16.
Mapping of the world according to the four quartiles of the longevity of the countries. Where quartile 1 is 0 to 67.25 years, quartile 2 is 67.3 to 74.15 years, quartile 3 is 74.2 to 78.125 years, and quartile 4 is 78.2 to 84.2 years.

the quartiles of both the variables, we attempted to make the comparison of both variables making it apparent. Quartiles were calculated with the help of the buvilt-in QUARTILE function of MS excel for each of the two data groups. The mapping was performed using the online tool provided by www.mapchart.net.

9. Discussion

In this chapter, we first had an overview of the biomedical innovations of the current times. We then hypothesized that these innovations may have a profound effect on the life expectancy and general health of the population. For this, we revisited the relationship of GDP per capita income to the life expectancy, taking GDP as the surrogate measure of the health facilities provided in the country. Our analyses included data for the past 10 years (2009–2018) for 183 countries.

These analyses targeted one key question: does life expectancy increase with increasing income?

Overall, the analysis of the GDP and life expectancy data of the past 10 years suggests a considerable correlation between income level and life expectancy. It is to be noted that biomedical innovations are more likely to be bought and utilized in countries with stronger economies and higher income levels. Hence, the longevity of their citizens increases. In contrast, the countries with poorer economies are unable to possess the latest biomedical innovation and hence have shorter lifespans and worse quality of life of their citizens.

As a future direction, the research and development (R&D) of biomedical technology should weigh in the factor of affordability and mass production. For this, the researches may opt for cheaper and locally available materials while building the end product. Also, the outsourcing of R&D and production of these technologies will create more employment options in developing countries.

10. Conclusion

The results of our analyses showed that there exists a direct positive relationship between per capita income and the expected years of life across countries. These results support our hypothesis that growth in the biomedical industry and a resultant growth in the healthcare industry will have a positive impact on the economy. This positive impact will improve the longevity of the people.

Author details

Samreen Hussain*, Sarmad Shams and Saad Jawaid Khan
Faculty of Engineering Science and Technology, Ziauddin University, Karachi, Pakistan

*Address all correspondence to: samreen.hussain18@gmail.com

References

[1] Harkins CS, McGarry A, Buis A. Provision of prosthetic and orthotic services in low-income countries: A review of the literature. Prosthetics and Orthotics International. 2013;**37**(5):353-361

[2] Phillips B, Zingalis G, Ritter S, Mehta K. A review of current upper-limb prostheses for resource constrained settings. In: Proc. 5th IEEE Glob. Humanit. Technol. Conf. GHTC 2015. 2015. pp. 52-58

[3] Cordella F et al. Literature review on needs of upper limb prosthesis users. Frontiers in Neuroscience. 2016;**10**:1-14

[4] Carrozza MC, Member A. Transradial Prosthesis; 2009

[5] Jones SF. The physiology of the joints. Physiotherapy. 1990;**76**(1):52

[6] Biddiss EA, Chau TT. Upper limb prosthesis use and abandonment: a survey of the last 25 years. Prosthetics and Orthotics International. 2007;**31**(3):236-257

[7] Micera S, Carpaneto J, Raspopovic S. Control of hand prostheses using peripheral information. IEEE Reviews in Biomedical Engineering. 2010;**3**:48-68

[8] Michael JW, Bowker JH. Atlas of Amputations and Limb Deficiencies: Surgical, Prosthetic, and Rehabilitation Principles. IL: American Academy of Orthopaedic Surgeons Rosemont; 2004

[9] Dianceht SA de CV. Cosmetic Prosthesis, Centro Medico Puerta de Hierro Sur. 2017. Available from: http://www.manosydedos.com/index_sel_dedos.html

[10] Plettenburg DH. The WILMER passive hand prosthesis for toddlers. Journal of Prosthetics and Orthotics. 2009;**21**(2):97-99

[11] OttoBock. Ottobock Health Care. 2017. Available from: http://www.ottobockus.com/prosthetics/upper-limb-prosthetics/solution-overview/body-powered-prosthetics/

[12] Northmore-Ball MD, Heger H, Hunter GA. The below-elbow myo-electric prosthesis. A comparison of the Otto bock myo-electric prosthesis with the hook and functional hand. Journal of Bone and Joint Surgery. British Volume. 1980;**62**(3):363-367

[13] Machado S, Almada LF, Annavarapu RN. Progress and prospects in EEG-based brain-computer interface: Clinical applications in neurorehabilitation. Journal of Rehabilitation Robotics. 2013;**1**(1):28-41

[14] Jiang N, Vujaklija I, Rehbaum H, Graimann B, Farina D. Is accurate mapping of EMG signals on kinematics needed for precise online myoelectric control? IEEE Transactions on Neural Systems and Rehabilitation Engineering. 2014;**22**(3):549-558

[15] Belter JT, Segil JL, Dollar AM, Weir RF. Mechanical design and performance specifications of anthropomorphic prosthetic hands: a review. Journal of Rehabilitation Research and Development. 2013;**50**(5):599-618

[16] ten Kate J, Smit G, Breedveld P. 3D-printed upper limb prostheses: A review. Disability and Rehabilitation Assistive Technology. 2017;**12**(3):300-314

[17] Bionics T. Touch Bionics Product Catalog. 2017. Available from: http://www.touchbionics.com/sites/default/files/files/Touch

[18] Yip BE. Review: Upper Limb Prostheses. Rochester, N.Y: Image; 2009

[19] Steeper RSL. BeBionic3 Product Brochure. 2012. Available from: http://bebionic.com/distributor/documents/bebionic3_technical_information_-_Lo_Res.pdf

[20] Waryck B. Comparison of two myoelectric multi-articulating prosthetic hands. In: Proc. 2011 Myoelectric Control. Prosthetics Symp. 2011. pp. 1-4

[21] Gmbh VS. First experiences with the Vincent hand. In: Schulz S, editor. Symp. A Q. J. Mod. Foreign Lit. 2011

[22] Schulz S, Spengel S, Probst P. New Strategies for Myoelectric Control of Multi-Articulating Hand and Partial Hand Prostheses; MEC'14 Redefining Norm, No. August 2014. pp. 215-218

[23] Johannes MS, Bigelow JD, Burck JM, Harshbarger SD, Kozlowski MV, Van Doren T. An overview of the developmental process for the modular prosthetic limb. Johns Hopkins APL Technical Digest (Applied Physics Laboratory). 2011;**30**(3):207-216

[24] Cheesborough JE, Dumanian GA, Smith LH, Kuiken TA. Targeted muscle reinnervation and advanced prosthetic arms. Seminars in Plastic Surgery. 2015;**29**(1):62-72

[25] Hebert JS et al. Novel targeted sensory reinnervation technique to restore functional hand sensation after transhumeral amputation. IEEE Transactions on Neural Systems and Rehabilitation Engineering. 2014;**22**(4):765-773

[26] Ravitz AD et al. Revolutionizing prosthetics-phase 3. Johns Hopkins APL Technical Digest (Applied Physics Laboratory). 2013;**31**(4):366-376

[27] Bennett DA, Member S, Dalley SA, Truex D, Goldfarb M. A multigrasp hand prosthesis for providing precision and conformal grasps. IEEE/ASME Transactions on Mechatronics. 2015;**20**(4):1697-1704

[28] Dalley SA, Member S, Bennett DA, Member S, Goldfarb M. Functional assessment of the vanderbilt multigrasp myoelectric hand: A continuing case study. Conference Proceedings: Annual International Conference of the IEEE Engineering in Medicine and Biology Society. 2014;**2014**:6195-6198

[29] Bionics O. Hero Arm. 2019. Available from: https://openbionics.com/hero-arm-user-guide

[30] Slade P, Akhtar A, Nguyen M, Bretl T. Tact: Design and Performance of an Open-Source, Affordable, Myoelectric Prosthetic Hand2015. pp. 6451-6456

[31] Bionics O. Ada Hand. 2016. Available from: https://www.openbionics.com/, Licens https://creativecommons.org/licenses/by-sa/4.0/

[32] Medynski C, Rattray B. Bebionic prosthetic design. In: MEC 2011 Symp. MyoElectric Control. Prosthetics Symp. 2011. pp. 1-4

[33] Cervellati M, Sunde U. Life expectancy and economic growth: The role of the demographic transition. Journal of Economic Growth. 2011;**16**(2):99-133

[34] Lichtenberg FR. Have newer cardiovascular drugs reduced hospitalization? Evidence from longitudinal country-level data on 20 OECD countries, 1995-2003. Health Economics. 2009;**18**(5):519-534

[35] Lichtenberg FR. The Contribution of Pharmaceutical Innovation to Longevity Growth in Germany and France; 2010

[36] Lichtenberg FR. Has pharmaceutical innovation reduced social security disability growth? International

Journal of the Economics of Business. 2011;**18**(2):293-316

[37] Lichtenberg FR. The effect of pharmaceutical innovation on the functional limitations of elderly Americans: Evidence from the 2004 National Nursing Home Survey. In: The Economics of Medical Technology. Bingley, United Kingdom: Emerald Group Publishing Limited; 2012. pp. 73-101

[38] Lichtenberg FR. The effect of pharmaceutical innovation on longevity: Patient level evidence from the 1996-2002 medical expenditure panel survey and linked mortality public-use files. In: Forum for Health Economics and Policy. Vol. 16. pp. 1-33

[39] Lichtenberg FR. The impact of new (orphan) drug approvals on premature mortality from rare diseases in the United States and France, 1999-2007. The European Journal of Health Economics. 2013;**14**(1):41-56

[40] Lichtenberg FR. The impact of pharmaceutical innovation on longevity and medical expenditure in France, 2000-2009. Economics and Human Biology. 2014;**13**:107-127

[41] Lichtenberg FR, Virabhak S. Pharmaceutical-Embodied Technical Progress, Longevity, and Quality of Life: Drugs as Equipment for your Health; 2002

[42] Cutler D, Deaton A, Lleras-Muney A. The determinants of mortality. The Journal of Economic Perspectives. 2006;**20**(3):97-120

[43] Kramarow E, Lubitz J, Lentzner H, Gorina Y. Trends in the health of older Americans, 1970-2005. Health Affairs. 2007;**26**(5):1417-1425

[44] Fuchs VR. New priorities for future biomedical innovations. The New England Journal of Medicine. 2010;**363**(8):704-706

[45] N. I. of Health. Impact of NIH Research on our Health; 2012

[46] Lichtenberg FR. The quality of medical care, behavioral risk factors, and longevity growth. International Journal of Health Care Finance and Economics. 2011;**11**(1):1-34

[47] MW Dictionary. Definition of Longevity

[48] Dorsey ER et al. Funding of US biomedical research, 2003-2008. The Journal of the American Medical Association. 2010;**303**(2):137-143

[49] Frenk J. Health and the Economy: A Vital Relationship: Healthcare Performance Is Strongly Dependent on the Economy, but Also on the Health Systems themselves. This Link Should Not be Underestimated; OECD Obs. No. 2432004. pp. 9-11

[50] Jetter M, Laudage S, Stadelmann D. The Intimate Link between Income Levels and Life Expectancy: Global Evidence from 213 Years; 2016

[51] Fund. I.M. World Economic Outlook database; 2018

[52] GeoBase. Life Expectancy; 2019

Chapter 3

Human-Computer/Device Interaction

Dagmawi Lemma Gobena

Abstract

Any interaction refers to the communication between two or more entities (be it abstract/conceptual or physical entity). Successful interaction is equated from the properties of each entity involved in the interaction as well as the capabilities of the interacting entities. With the diversified use and application of computers and specialized devices for specific tasks, such as biomechanical and biomedical devices, interaction design needs to further study the context of the tasks as well. Moreover, with the inclusion of embedded systems and smart devices, instead of focusing only on the hardware performance, the computer architecture needs to consider the opportunities. Especially, HCI can be improved as the current technologies are giving an opportunity for building smart interaction where the user interacts with devices implicitly and in less obtrusive way. In light of this, the design and architecture of an engineered product need to strive for making the product usable and used while making it useful to the user. And this can be achieved if interaction design is dictated by scrutinizing the user model with respects to the usability attributes in view of the context of its task as well as the platform capabilities and constraints as discussed in this chapter.

Keywords: interaction design, user-centered design, user interface, implicit interaction, HCI, CHI

1. Introduction

It used to be the case, in the mid-1990s, where people use computers only as a means to analyze and calculate sophisticated mathematical, statistical, and/or scientific problems. By then, the design and architecture of computers used to focus on the computational performance and/or storage capacity. By then, computer architecture was more concerned with the set of rules and methods to describe the functionalities of various components and how these components are organized in the implementation of computer systems to achieve better performance.

In view of "better performance," often computer engineers consider improved processing speed, storage capacity, and information retrieval. Otherwise, interaction performance, associated with the user, used to be less considered. This perspective cannot persist after the introduction of personal computers and especially with the proliferation of mobile technologies like smartphones. If the design and architecture consider only the internal architecture of the functionalities of the components, aiming to address data processing and storage requirements only, but not the user profile nor the context of the users' tasks, usability could be compromised.

Often, computer architecture is much concerned with the performance of the device so as to effectively and efficiently execute users' tasks regardless of the user itself. Instead, users are expected to learn how to use the device architecture and comply with the limitation of the platform while executing their task/s. Such consideration is, of course, rooted to the assumptions of the known user profile of the first-generation computers, where a single group of people used to design, build, program, operate, and maintain each machine [1].

After the introduction of personal computers, and when computers become an indispensable and useful machine for everyone, the functions that can be performed by computers and devices were abstracted at the software layer so as to mediate the interaction language between the machine and the human-user. Particularly, the user interface of software (i.e., application software) determines how users can communicate with the device so as to access a particular service in a machine.

As shown in **Figure 1**, though users actually interact physically with a device, they actually require it to execute a use case to accomplish their need. Hence, users are interacting logically with the service. Software engineers define the service as a use case that is realized by a certain subsystem/component in the software, while the interface is considered as boundary class during analysis and as the user interface during the design and implementation stage.

As the performance of the user is also important to benefit the improved performance of the computer/machine, the user interface design process (usability engineering) takes due consideration to understand the machine. As a result, one of the important tasks in usability engineering lifecycle is scrutinizing the platform capabilities and constraints [2–4]. The platform capabilities are used to meet users' requirements [5] but are limited as specified in the respective architecture of the computer/device. Similarly, the constraints are the result of the architectural organization of the components in the device.

A software that is designed to run on a certain machine (platform), as it benefits from the capabilities of the computer/devices, also could be limited in having some desired functionalities because of the constraints associated with the device architecture. Thus, the human-computer interaction (HCI) further needs to identify and/create interaction modality to complement the limitations while complying with the architectural description of the machine. Such approaches may enable and support users to effectively and efficiently execute their use cases (tasks/functions) on the constrained platform.

With the diversified use and application of computers and specialized devices for specific tasks, such as biomechanical and biomedical devices, the interaction design needs to further study the context of the tasks as well. Moreover, with the

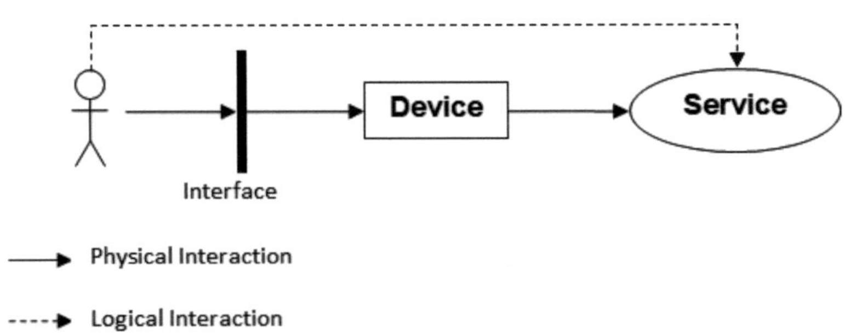

Figure 1.
Interaction between user, device, and service.

DOI: http://dx.doi.org/10.5772/intechopen.86673

inclusion of embedded systems and smart devices, instead of focusing only on the hardware performance, smart technologies shall be considered as opportunities in the design of HCI, so that user interface/interaction designers can easily and systematically assimilate user interaction modalities in the devices.

In this chapter, we provide HCI basics first and then discuss the process of effective HCI development. Finally, we introduce the broad categories of HCI, explicit and implicit, in view of recent computational models and embedded systems, which are an integral part of specific purpose computer system as in vehicles and industrial, biomechanical, and biomedical devices/machines.

2. HCI basics

Lately, when computers of the fourth generation evolve and as application software became indispensable resource and widely used, software engineers use the term "user-friendly" in connection with the interaction and to denote how the software is convenient for users. However, this term is not appropriate for various reasons as indicated in [3], and it is not measurable. Technically, it may imply the consideration of a single dimension of user profile and users' needs, while indeed users' profile and needs are heterogeneous.

When supporting the user performance became equally important to computer performance, alternative terms like usability, user experience, end-user criteria, etc. are coined. In line with user interface design, the field evolved as HCI studying the interaction between the computer/devices and the human-user.

HCI primarily focuses on improving the user performance and satisfaction during interactions the users encounter with the computer/device. Though the "C" in the abbreviation "HCI" refers to the word "computer," technically it must mean both the hardware and software. And, by hardware, we mean any device or machine, or it may simply refer the device, which is an engineered product. But, since software is also an integral part of a computer system, in the following sections, by "engineering product" we mean the device or the software—or both.

2.1 Goals of HCI

Whether the interaction is with the hardware part of computer (machine or device) or the software, the goal of HCI design is to improve the usefulness, usability, and/or usedness of the engineered product [6]. It is also important to provide an intuitive and natural interaction experience for the user [7], so as to make the product acceptable by the user.

The acceptability of the product can have technical or social aspect [7] or the combination of both [3]. Though such classification of acceptability could be useful for simplifying the understanding, some of the attributes considered to measure the practical acceptability could be closely related to social acceptability.

A product's acceptability is related to usefulness of the product [8]. Nielsen [3] considers usefulness as "practical" acceptability, which in turn is divided into two categories, "utility" and "usability."

While utility is associated with meeting the functionality of the product, usability can further take a multidimensional concern, and it could be important to support more than single user, and this forms community subjected to social value [9]. Yet, satisfaction, which is considered as one of the practical usability metrics, could greatly affect the social acceptability. For instance, users could just simply dislike the product.

2.1.1 Usefulness and usedness

A useful engineered product (hardware/software) needs to meet the user requirement. That is, the product shall help the user to accomplish its task/s.

Users primarily desire to accomplish their task, which is the functional requirement, through the interaction they undertake with the engineered product. Having the notion of utility then, which is also, among the end-user design goal criteria [10], HCI focuses on the construction of effective interaction so as to make the computer useful to the user.

Usefulness is related to the perceived value of the product. That is, how users interact with the engineered product is not an inhibitor to the adoption of an engineered product if its value is high [11]. It has to be noted that if a product is useful, the user might need to learn how to use it, even if learning the product could be difficult. Also, even after learning the "useful" product, which has high utility value, the interaction with the product might not be pleasing or safe or both. Hence, the goal of HCI includes production of usable products—making the useful product usable.

2.1.2 Usability

In the case where an engineered product is useful but not usable, usability could often be compensated through trainings and technical supports. When a useful product is possible to affect the operation or safety of the user, it is common to use precaution mark or dialogs, such as warning or disclaimer, so that the user may use the product with care but with his/her own risk.

If the motor capability inhibits the user from operating a product that is perceived useful (e.g., due to disability), then supplementing the user's physical limitation through additional accessories could be vital. For example, due to stroke, a user might be unable to control his/her fingers as usual. Such people, therefore, will experience difficulty with interactions that may require keyboard use and typing due to their limited motor skills of the hands and fingers. Hence, it is important to consider assistive typing or Typing aid, as shown in **Figure 2**, for improving the performance of the user.

Construction of a device and computer system needs to take into consideration on how users interact with it. While performing their task using the engineered product as utility, it is preferred to support users to interact with the engineered

Figure 2.
Use of typing aid for improving typing accuracy for people with limited motor skills of the hands and fingers [12].

product easily, naturally, safely, and securely [6]. Hence, producing a usable product is one of the HCI goals.

Usability is not a one-dimensional attribute of an engineered product; rather it comprises several components that can sometimes conflict; hence, interaction designers need to trade off between the various quality attributes. In order to trade off between important usability attributes and/or construct usable product, it is important to study and understand the human needs as well as ability. Hence, understanding the physical, cognitive, perceptual, personality, and cultural differences [9] of users to whom the product is engineered is important.

While computer design and architecture focus on improving the performance of the hardware, nowadays, it is important to consider the performance of the user as well who would use the product. Such consideration will make the product usable; and usability engineering strives to attain it.

The user performance is associated with various usability attributes. Models have been suggested to understand and represent the user performance so as to apply it during the construction of usable product and latter to qualitatively and quantitatively evaluate the engineered product.

The level of the focus bestowed to the various usability attributes may overlap and/or vary in scope. In fact, as usability is getting universal acceptance, the attributes considered in various models are increasing. For example, the usability consideration in the ISO 9241-11 covers three attributes (effectiveness, efficiency, and satisfaction) in 1998. Then, in 3 years, in the ISO 9126 model, extended model has been proposed to include and clarify the concern into understandability, learnability, operability, attractiveness, and even compliance to standard.

The usability consideration is also evolving along with the improving performance of engineered products and is becoming diversified. Those models which are proposed to simplify usability concern by grouping usability attributes are documented in [13]. These attributes can be useful to systematically capture the physical, cognitive, perceptual, personality, and cultural differences of users.

The usability attributes are useful to objectively measure the interaction design from motor capability, psychological makeup, perceptual and cognitive model, and experience and expectation perspectives of users. Yet, as interaction is not one directional, it is possible that the engineered product could affect the user performance. Following, we have summarized the attributes, shown in **Figure 3**, in alignment with psychological, motor capability, and perceptual and cognition model of the user.

Perceptual and cognitive model of the user: Aligning the design and architecture of engineered product toward the perceptual and cognition model (or mental model) of the user would help to easily engage the user; and the more a user is engaged and utilizes the product, the more he/she learns and understands it.

A product that is easy to understand and learn would improve the user experience [14]. Users' performance, as well, will improve as they learn the product and when time passes by using the product. Thus, learning and understanding the product is important to improve the performance and experience of the user.

The important attributes considered in various usability models are grouped and described as shown in **Table 1**. We took learnability, from Nielson, Shackel, ISO 9126, and Eason model [3, 15, 16], understandability from the ISO 9126 standard, and memorability from Nielson's model [3] as attributes that belong to the perceptual and cognitive dimension.

Psychological makeup of the user: Even if users are physically able to interact with an engineered product, it may not be always the case that they will be willing or interested in using it. Why users might dislike the product or be anxious about it, why users are not motivated to use the product or attracted to, and why users are not eager to use the product are not necessarily related to the usefulness of the

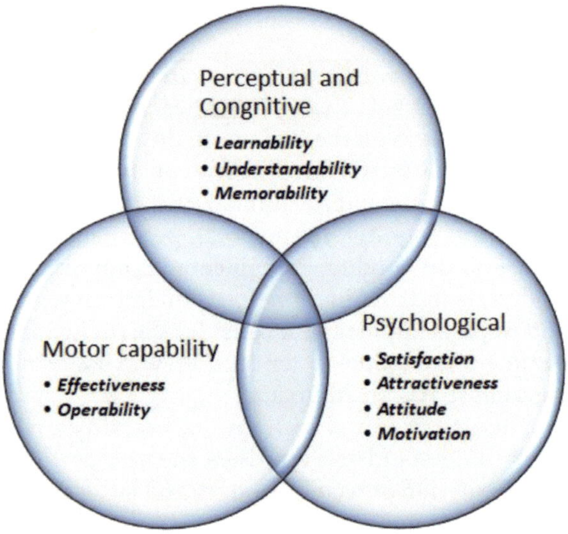

Figure 3.
Usability dimensions and related attributes.

Attribute	Description
Learnability	As an engineered product becomes usable, it would have the benefit of reducing training and supports to the end user. This usability attribute can also be considered as a scale for measuring the effort the end user needs to learn the system
Understandability	This attribute is a supplement to learnability as it determines the ease of which the systems' functions can be indeed understood by the user
Memorability	This is a more desired attribute and primary usability goal in areas where users are casual types. That is, when users are expected to use the system casually, then the system should be easy to remember

Table 1.
Usability attributes related to perceptual and cognition model of the user.

product. Even people, who enjoy using computers, may have very different preferences for interaction styles during usage of specific application in the computer [9].

Rather some usability attributes, which can affect the user performance (directly or indirectly), could be related to psychological makeup of the user. The satisfaction attribute used in Nielson's model [3] and ISO 9241-11 [17], attractiveness from (ISO 9126), attitude from the Shackel's definition of usability [15], and motivation from Eason et al. [16, 18] can be grouped into psychological scale as detailed in **Table 2**.

Motor capability of user: Motor capability refers to the physical orientation of a user. The user's engagement depends on his/her motor capability toward operating the machinery. This encourages the user to improve the understanding about the engineered product with which he/she interacts with [19]. Therefore, it is useful to understand and model user's ability as well as disability. From the engineered product's perspective, the operability of the product and the effectiveness of the user in performing a task are the major attributes considered from the motor capability dimension, as discussed under **Table 3**.

2.2 The building blocks

Having a multidimensional perspective of HCI, such as the mental, psychological, and physical dimensions, profiling the user is important since users can have

Attribute	Description
Satisfaction	This attribute is associated with acceptability of the engineered product by the user as the product is pleasant to use, in a specified context of use, so that the user is subjectively satisfied with it
Attractiveness	This attribute is related to the look and feel of the engineered product. As "beauty is in the eye of the beholder," meeting this requirement could be challenging, especially when the personality of users is diverse. Hence, applying multiple interaction styles/methods could be vital
Attitude	Shackel [15] defines this psychological attribute as "the acceptance of users with their levels of discomfort, tiredness, frustration and personal effort." It has to be noted that users do not always operate the engineered product in a silent and comfortable environment. Some environments might create additional stress and distraction, while the frequency of the distraction may also vary
Motivation	This refers to the determination of the user in using the engineered product for completing the task. Some projects deliver useful products, but users might "just" disregard it and may prefer to stick to old trends. In some cases, attractive engineered products (e.g., smart phone) might improve the motivation of the user, which is associated with design solution. Yet, other solutions, such as rewarding the user might be useful. For example, Ethiopian Airlines, when it first introduced online flight booking, offered 2% discount for those who book online, and this could be one strategy to motivate using the system—on which the company invested. Otherwise, if the system is not well used, the entire investment on the production of the given system could be a waste

Table 2.
Usability attributes related to the psychological makeup of the user.

Attribute	Description
Operability	Engineered product shall enable the user to operate and control it. But how much the user can control the product and the degree of usage is associated with the motor capability of the user
Effectiveness	Associated with the user's accomplishment of a specified task or goal successfully timely, it is also performance measurement of specific user groups. The effective utilization of the engineered product is directly related to the user's physical capability; hence, we associate it with motor capability

Table 3.
Usability attributes related to motor capability of user.

their own capabilities and constraints. Once the user profile is defined, setting goals to be achieved in the construction of the interaction modality and in alignment of the users' profile is important. For example, visually receiving information could be a capability of the user yet can be constrained by the visual acuity.

A successful design solution of HCI shall also be associated with the platform (which can be hardware or software) and need to consider the context of the user task. Hence, platform capabilities and constraints are determinants to meet the goal of HCI. The platform capabilities considered in the design of a certain engineered product shall be in alignment to the capability of the user. Likewise, the identified user capability shall help the design decision during the selection between various competitive platforms. For example, an industrial machine to be operated with touch screen interface is usable for users with hand/s and who are not visually impaired.

The user and platform are two of the building blocks that need due consideration to meet the goals of HCI; and the task is the third block. By "task," we mean the use case that is meaningful in the system under construction. The measurement of a particular task accomplishment is related to the context of the environment in general. For example, performing a task in a destructive environment and silent environment requires different design consideration in building successful HCI. Hence, HCI needs to take into account the context of the task as well as the environment where the task should be executed.

Furthermore, a user might be able to accomplish a particular task effectively and efficiently if it knows how to initiate the task, how the task used to be known in one environment (e.g., real-world environment) is represented in the newly developed product (e.g., computer/virtual environment), and how the engineered product gives feedback when the task is completed. In this regard, interaction design shall apply appropriate metaphor selection and application.

3. Command and feedback

The goals of HCI can be meet by undertaking engineering process that may result with effective and usable two-way communication between the user and the engineered product. This two-way communication often appears as a command issued by the end user and feedback responded by the product.

The mode of command determines how the user easily issues the instruction to the engineered product while using it. This is further associated with the motor capability of the user as discussed above. For example, in the design of biomechanical systems, as biomechanics focus on the structure and function of the mechanical aspects of biological systems, the motor capability of the user would be vital in the design consideration, among other usability factors discussed above. However, since the interaction is a two-way communication, it is also important to properly design the feedback of the engineered product, in such a way the feedback can be well received and understood by the end user.

Users expect adequate feedback about their actions and ways of easily checking the status [9] of the task they are executing. Feedback has traditionally been seen as a responsive facility to be a communication of immediate system state to the end user [20].

The effectiveness of the feedback from the system is equated to the appropriate selection from tones of interaction styles, where the selection is based on the user, task, and platform model. That means:

- The persona needs to allow the user to receive and understand the feedback.
- The feedback needs to be produced in the context of the task and with the consideration of the task environment.
- The platform (the engineered product) needs to have the capability to produce the feedback.

Renaud and Cooper [20] classify feedback as archival and immediate. Archival feedback, primarily, is related to information about past activity such as a history of both the user's actions, together with the system's response. It can also be considered "similar to an instruction manual or a system overview that allows users to preview system operations" [21]. Whereas, immediate feedback is used to communicate the present state of the system and involves real-time prompts [21]. In both types of feedbacks presented in [20], the interaction design considers modeling the user so that the user can receive the feedback well, while the assumption is that the user interacts with the system explicitly.

4. Explicit versus implicit interaction

In the customary computing models, users are expected to interact with the system (engineered product) explicitly—hence explicit HCI (e-HCI). In the case of e-HCI, the interaction design aims to design and present the engineer product in such a way users know the presence of the product, and they should learn and understand how to interact with the product. Hence, it is required to design the computer-to-the-user.

However, as the result of smart computing models like ubiquitous computing, where the interaction is desired to be implicit, the notion of the command and feedback design might requires to designing the user-to-the-computer as well so as to enable the computer perceive the context of the user [22]—leading to implicit HCI (i-HCI) [6].

Weiser's vision of ubiquitous computing, which demands that computer to be an invisible servant [23, 24], can be realized if the user interacts with the engineered product less obtrusively. This is also pertinent in designing smart devices that improve the efficiency and automation of industrial devices.

Also, with regard to HCI, invisibility of computers can be achieved, partly through i-HCI [22] and context-aware systems. On the other hand, in addition to providing natural interaction (such as speech and gesture), the e-HCI development for interactive ubiquitous systems requires consideration of capabilities and constraints of heterogeneous platforms and users. Hence, the designers and developers are often compelled to configure and integrate heterogeneous platforms to meet needs of ubiquitous computing, such as mobility and implicit interaction. Therefore, both considerations of designing the-user-to-computer and the computer-to-the-user might be required.

In interactive systems where the user interacts with the engineered product explicitly, the user needs to have the model of the system. Thus, the interaction design focuses on crafting the computer/device, assuming the user will understand the presence of the engineered product, and it can operate it with its motor capability. Thus, the focus is more about the human-to-computer (H2C) interaction.

For example, consider a user who conducts quality inspection in a manufacturing process while the item is being manufactured, the item might need to pass over a conveyor belt. The user (inspector) needs a control over the conveyor—from turning on/off the conveyor to speed control. Thus, the user needs to explicitly access the control panel. In such case, the important usability consideration for the interaction design is positioning the control panel using the right metaphors for the interface. Otherwise, the user would have the knowledge on the existence of the control panel and the associated buttons/switches. Yet the design of the control panel shall consider various usability attributes discussed in Section 2.

Alternatively, the interaction could be computer-to-human. For example (considering the example in the preceding paragraph), instead of requiring the user to directly manipulate the control panel, the conveyor could be designed to be smart and know the absence/presence of the user (inspector) might take actions autonomously or advise the user on favorable actions. This approach makes the interaction implicit.

In i-HCI, the presence of the user in the computing model is not primarily to interact with the product. But, the presence can be sensed by the computer, and the computer shall take actions (give feedback to the user) based on previously or dynamically modeled user's context. Implicit interaction is based on the assumption that the engineered product, with which the user interacts, has a certain understanding of users' behavior and action in a given situations being a user-aware [6]. Thus, the design and architecture of the engineered product need to consider additional components (such as sensors and actuators) other than the components useful to attain the functional operations.

5. Conclusion

Any engineered product is designed and constructed with the intention of solving user's problem, often, through improvement of the user performance and capacity. And the users need to interact with the product in order to utilize it for accessing the service/s or functionality/functionalities provided by the respective product.

The interaction between the user and the product is primarily for addressing the user's problem which is associated with the usefulness of the engineered product. But the usefulness of the product is only one aspect. Otherwise, the acceptability of the product is associated with the usability and usedness of the product as well. Therefore, considering computer/device as an engineered product, the design and architecture of any engineered product shall give due consideration for the design of human-computer/device interaction.

First and foremost, as a user is one who operates and interacts with engineered product; it is important to properly profile the user considering the user's motor capability, psychological makeup, as well as the perceptual and cognitive model. Secondly, as the engineered product, which eventually interacts with the user, would be constructed over a certain platform and set of technologies, it is worth to consider the capabilities and constraints of the platform over which the product is designed or the product itself. Therefore, the understanding of the user as well as the platform capabilities and constraints would help to consider the right types of interaction modalities.

Also, in the design and architecture of an engineered product, in today's technology and with the emerging needs of smart computing, interaction design might lead to the design of implicit interaction between the product and the user. This, in turn, requires integration of various technologies such as RFID, sensors, and actuators to build smartness in the engineered product. Hence, the design and architecture of engineered product need to take into account the specification and organization of additional components beyond the ones used for processing the functional requirements and storing the information produced in relation to the task.

Author details

Dagmawi Lemma Gobena
Addis Ababa University, Ethiopia

*Address all correspondence to: dagmawi.lemma@aau.edu.et

References

[1] Andrew S. Tanenbaum Modern Operating Systems. 4th ed. New Jersey: Pearson Education; 2015

[2] Mayhew D. The Usability Engineering Lifecycle. San Francisco: Morgan Kaufmann Publishers; 1999

[3] Nielsen J. Usability Engineering. London, San Diego: Morgan Kaufmann; 1993

[4] Ratner J, editor. Human Factors and Web Development. 2nd ed. New Jersey: Taylor & Francis e-Library; 2009

[5] Magno Q , Paul T, Tim C, Rajeev S. Corporate knows best (maybe): The impact of global versus local IT capabilities on business unit agility. In: Proceedings of the 51st Hawaii International Conference on System Sciences (HICSS); 2-6 January 2018. Hawaii, USA: HiCSS; 2018. p. 5212-5221

[6] Posland S. Ubiquitous Computing: Smart Device, Environment, and Interactions. Chicester, UK: John Wilesy & Sons Ltd; 2009

[7] Dong Wu, Jianhua G, Yi Li. Interaction technology based on 3D printing topographics and table for emergency management. In: Proceedings of the 2018 2nd International Conference on Big Data and Internet of Things (BDIOT 2018); 24-26 October 2018; Beijing, China: ACM; 2018. p. 100-104

[8] Giovanny A, Auguste R, Eric B. Improving users' product acceptability: An approach based on Bayesian networks and a simulated annealing algorithm. International Journal of Production Research. 2016;**54**(17):1-18

[9] Shneiderman B, Plaisant C, Cohen M, Jacobs S, Elmqvist N, Diakopoulos N. Designing the User Interface: Strategies for Effective Human-Computer Interaction. 6th ed. Harlow: Pearson Education; 2018

[10] Bruegge B, Dutoit A. Object Oriented Software Engineering: Using UML, Patterns and Java. 3rd ed. Harlow: Prentice Hall; 2014

[11] Derrett N. Heckel's law: Conclusions from the user interface design of a music appliance—the bassoon: Pers Ubiquit Comput. 2004;**8**(3-4):208-212

[12] www.sportaid.com. [Online]. https://www.sportaid.com/typing-aid.html

[13] Madan A, Kumar S. Usability evaluation methods—A literature review: International Journal of Engineering Science and Technology (IJEST). 2012;**4**(2):590-599

[14] Allison G, Michael A. When cognition interferes with innovation: Overcoming cognitive obstacles to design thinking; research. Technology Management. 2018;**61**(4):45-51

[15] Shackel B. Usability – Context, framework, definition, design and evaluation. Interacting with Computers. 2009;**21**(5-6):339-346

[16] Eason K. Towards the experimental study of usability. Behaviour & Information Technology. 1984;**3**(2):133-143

[17] Nigel B, James C, Susan H. ISO 9241-11 revised: What have we learnt about usability since 1998? In: Human-Computer Interaction: Design and Evaluation. Vol. 9169. Cham: Springer; 2015

[18] Tomayess I, Pedro I. Usability and human computer interaction (HCI). In: Sustainable Design. London: Springer; 2015

[19] Vladimir R. The old media in the new media: A comparative. International Journal of Performance Arts and Digital Media. 2019;**15**:23-24

[20] Renaud K, Cooper R. Feedback in human-computer interaction—characteristics and recommendations. 2000;**26**:105-114

[21] Chiang P, Chang H, Chang Y. PotteryGo: A virtual pottery making training system. IEEE Computer Graphics and Applications. 2018;**38**(2):74-88

[22] Page T, Gisli T. Emerging technologies in interaction with mobile computing devices—A technology forecast. i-manager's Journal on Mobile Applications and Technologies. 2018;**5**(1):1-14

[23] Adam G. Everyware: The Dawning Age of Ubiquitous Computing. Berkeley, USA: New Riders Publishing; 2006

[24] Weiser M. The computer for the 21st century. Scientific American. 1991;**263**(3):94-104

Chapter 4

Artificial Intelligence in Light-Source Design

Snjezana Soltic and Andrew N. Chalmers

Abstract

The advent of light-emitting diode (LED) light sources has led to a new freedom in the design of light-source spectra, and it is now possible to optimise for different source performance parameters, which is the principal aim of the authors' work. LEDs and lasers are real or potential light sources, and are inherently monochromatic, that is, narrow-band sources, with typical optical bandwidths in the range 20–40 nm (nanometres) for LEDs and 1–5 nm for diode lasers. Mixtures of three or more can be used to produce nominally white light of the type acceptable for general purpose lighting. It is a characteristic of all types of sources that there is a trade-off between good colour properties and high efficiencies, and the methods described here are directed towards an optimum combination of such parameters. This chapter will explain the use of differential evolution (DE) as a highly effective heuristic approach to optimisation, and proceeds to explain the structure and operation of a DE algorithm designed as an optimisation tool for such purposes.

Keywords: differential evolution, optimisation, LED lighting, luminous efficacy, correlated colour temperature, colour rendering and fidelity

1. Introduction

It has been stated by some authors that white LEDs are the eco-friendly light sources for the twenty-first century [1]. White light in LEDs can be produced either (i) by using blue (or violet) light to irradiate a phosphor that emits yellow light [2, 3] or (ii) by combining the outputs of a group of monochromatic LEDs [1, 4, 5]. In approach (i) the blue or violet is combined with the yellow to produce white light. We have adopted approach (ii) in which three (or, preferably, four) primary colours are mixed in appropriate proportions to produce high-quality white light with higher efficiency than approach (i) since there is no loss of energy as in the down-conversion in the phosphor [5, 6]. Both approaches aim to design LED-based white-light sources characterised by high colour rendering and fidelity properties combined with high luminous efficacy. It is an established fact in light-source design that these two qualities are generally contravariant, and that both depend on the emitted spectrum of the source. We have found that fine-tuning of the intensities of the individual sources, as well as the selection of their individual peak wavelengths, enables us to define the best balance of the significant spectral properties of the mixture. Our adopted optimisation technique implements a trial-and-error search algorithm within an n-dimensional space $\{I_1, \ldots, I_i, \ldots, I_n\}$ until an acceptable spectral power distribution (SPD) is found for the white-light mixture [5, 7, 8].

IntechOpen

In this chapter, we will describe an approach to the design of the optimum LED mixture using a simple global optimisation algorithm based on differential evolution (DE) as proposed by Storn and Price [9]. We have optimised the SPDs of mixtures of real and simulated LEDs and diode lasers. For this purpose, a MATLAB program was developed that optimises the SPD of an arbitrary mixture of individual SPDs. Specific versions of this program were developed to implement several different techniques for defining (and calculating) the colour properties of sources.

This chapter proceeds as follows. In Section 2, the principles of the DE algorithm are described in detail. In Section 3, the theory of colour rendering and luminous efficacy is given, along with other relevant lighting terms and their usage. Section 4 presents a selection of key experimental results and comparisons and, finally, we state our conclusions in Section 5.

2. Differential evolution

Differential evolution is a powerful population-based evolutionary algorithm suitable for the optimisation of real-value multi-modal non-linear and non-differentiable objective functions $f_o(x_1, x_2, ..., x_n)$ [9, 10]. DE is simple and has proven to be powerful in solving a number of benchmark problems [11, 12].

The search for an optimal solution starts with a population of P randomly created solution vectors $\{v_1, v_2, ..., v_P\}$. This population is maintained constant during the optimisation process, during which the solution vectors (i.e., candidate SPDs) undergo mutation, crossover, evaluation and selection over a number of generations G. The best choices for both the population size P and the number of generations G depend on the problem to be optimised. Storn and Price suggest $P \in [5n, 10n]$, where n is the dimension of the objective function, but P must be ≥ 4 to provide sufficient mutually different solution vectors for the algorithm to function properly [10].

The operation of the algorithm is controlled by the use of a fitness function f_{fit} designed to discriminate between solutions (SPDs here) with 'good' or 'poor' properties.

Mutation is the process of creating a new offspring vector $u_{i,G+1}$ by adding the weighted difference between two randomly chosen solution vectors, $v_{r2,G}$ and $v_{r3,G}$, to a randomly chosen $v_{r1,G}$ [10]:

$$u_{i,G+1} = v_{r1,G} + F \times (v_{r2,G} - v_{r3,G}) \tag{1}$$

where F is a mutation weight $\in [0,2]$ and random indices $r_1, r_2, r_3 \in [0, P-1]$ are chosen to be different from the index i. The mutation process is illustrated in **Figure 1**.

The offspring solution vectors $u_{i,G+1}$ undergo crossover which ensures that the offspring vectors $w_{ji,G+1}$ differ from their parents [10]:

$$w_{ji,G+1} = \begin{cases} u_{ji,G+1} & \text{if } (j \leq CR) \mid (j = i) \\ v_{ji,G} & \text{if } (j > CR) \mid (j \neq i) \end{cases} \tag{2}$$

where the terms and parameters are defined as follows: $i \in \{1,2,..., P\}$ is a randomly chosen integer, $j \in [0, 1)$ is a randomly chosen real value, $CR \in [0, 1]$ is a crossover constant influencing the number of elements to be exchanged. An example of the crossover process is shown in **Figure 2**.

The process compares the offspring vectors $\{w_{1,G+1},..., w_{P,G+1}\}$ against their parent vectors $\{v_{1,G},..., v_{P,G}\}$. If the offspring $w_{i,G+1}$ has a better fitness function f_{fit} than its parent $v_{i,G}$, then it becomes a member of the next generation, $G + 1$. If not,

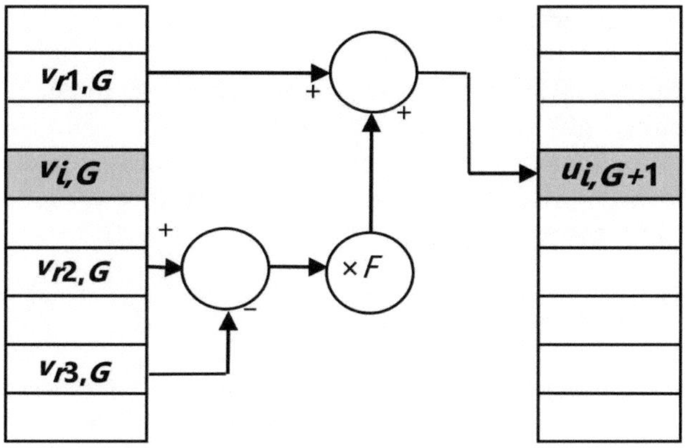

Figure 1.
Illustration of the mutation process for P = 9.

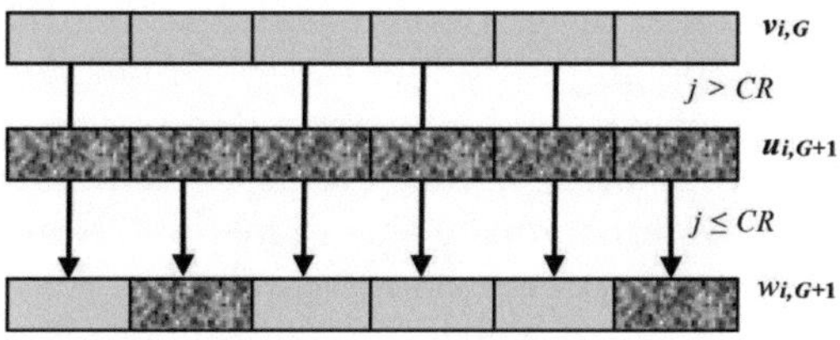

Figure 2.
Illustration of a typical crossover process for P = 6.

the $v_{i,G}$ vector is retained. Hence, only the fitter offspring become members of the $G + 1$ generation.

Proposals have been made for several variants of the original DE algorithm [10]. The most significant differences are in the creation of new solution vectors where:

1. the best solution vector from the current generation $v_{best,G}$ is mutated rather than $v_{r1,G}$;

2. more than two difference vectors are used in mutation; and

3. different crossover schemes are employed.

Our work is based on the original DE, and is described in pseudo-code given below:

```
Require: G, P, F ∈[0,2], CR ∈[0,1]
Create vectors {v1,0,...,vP,0}
Evaluate {v1,0,...,vP,0}->ffit,0
for all G do
  Mutate vi,G -> ui,G+1
  Crossover {u1,G+1,...,uP,G+1} and
    {v1,G,...,vP,G}->{w1,G+1,...,wP,G+1}
  Evaluate {w1,G+1,...,wP,G+1}
  if ffit(wi,G+1) > ffit(vi,G)
      vi,G+1 = wi,G+1
  else
      vi,G+1 = vi,G
  end if
end for
```

3. Light-source properties

Our purpose in this chapter is to present an approach to intelligent spectral design for any white-light source, aiming to achieve an optimum combination of luminous efficacy and colour rendering which, as previously noted, are contravariant characteristics of the SPD. We next introduce a brief outline of these, and other important, source properties.

3.1 Colour rendering index

Colour rendering has been defined by the *Commission Internationale de l'Éclairage*, International Commission on Illumination (CIE) who have published recommendations for the method of calculation of their colour rendering index (CRI) [13] based on a knowledge of the light-source spectrum. It represents an evaluation of the average colour shift of eight defined moderate-chroma colour samples when compared under the test source and a reference source having the same correlated colour temperature (CCT).[1] The system includes 14 test colours in total, and the additional 6 comprise 4 highly saturated colours (red, yellow, green, and blue) plus samples representing skin and foliage colours, respectively. As of the time of writing, this is the internationally agreed method. Note that CRI and associated technology have also been covered in [14]. The two most widely quoted colour rendering terms are: R_a—the general colour rendering index, based on the colour shifts of the eight principal test colour samples; and R_9—the 'special' (individual) index for the highly saturated red colour (sample 9).

In our optimisation work (see Section 4.1), we also made use of several derived indices symbolised as R_b, R_c and R_{min}, based, respectively, on: the 6 additional test colours; the full set of 14 test colours and the minimum individual value from the R_c set.

3.2 Colour fidelity index

Some dissatisfaction with the CIE method has arisen since the widespread adoption of LED lighting. As a consequence, the Illumination Engineering Society of North America (IES) has adopted a recommended method (TM-30-15) [15, 16] which recommends two new indices (R_f and R_g) for the classification of the colour properties of light sources. The underpinning research leading to the development of TM-30-15 [16–18] identified several weaknesses in the CIE's earlier CRI method [13], claiming that it does not adequately sample wavelength space and hence tends to over-estimate colour performance.

The method is also based on the colour-shift concept, but now using a set of 99 test colours considered to provide uniformity of both wavelength sampling and colour-space sampling. In addition, it uses a more modern colour-difference calculation technique, CAM02UCS [19] which is a development of the basic CIECAM02 colour appearance space [20].

The new index R_f gives an overall assessment of colour fidelity, while gamut index R_g indicates the relative magnitudes of colour shifts for sample colours in different regions of colour space. Also available is the skin colour index, $R_{f\,skin}$, which is an average of two specific sample-colour indices, selected as representative of human skin. In our optimisations, we also called up the minimum value of R_f,

---

[1] Defined in Section 3.5.

symbolised as $R_{f\,min}$, from the full set of 99 individual indices $R_{f\,i}$, as well as the referenced colour sample number i_{min} (in the set i_1 to i_{99}).

3.3 Colour quality scale

This was a precursor to TM-30-15, first proposed by Davis and Ohno of NIST (USA) [21]. The following serves as a brief introduction for the purpose of the present discussion. Again using the previously mentioned colour-shift concept, the CQS metric employs 15 saturated test colour samples, on the premise that certain light sources may render saturated colours more poorly than the de-saturated colours of the CIE's CRI method. The chromatic differences are calculated using the CIE 1976 (CIELAB) colour model [22].

The full calculation procedure has also been explained in [23]. It employs multiple steps, several of which are non-linear, resulting in the general CQS index, Q_a. As with the previous two cases, the 'special CQS' (Q_i) for each test colour sample may be calculated for a more thorough investigation of a test source. We have used the minimum value of Q_i (designated Q_{min}) from the set of 15 Q_i values, as an optimisation parameter.

3.4 Luminous efficacy of radiation

The luminous efficacy of the radiation (LER) of a light source assesses the 'lighting content' of the spectrum by comparing the visible light output (in lumens) to the total radiant output (in watts) as in Eq. 3.

$$LER = \frac{K_m \int_\lambda V(\lambda)S(\lambda)d\lambda}{\int_\lambda S(\lambda)d\lambda} \tag{3}$$

where K_m is the maximum luminous efficacy of radiation (≈683 lumen per watt), $S(\lambda)$ is the spectral distribution of the light source, and $V(\lambda)$ is the CIE spectral sensitivity function for human photopic vision [24]. The LER is an important determinant of the overall economy of a light source since the overall luminous efficacy is given by the product of LER with the energy conversion efficiency of the particular light source.

3.5 Correlated colour temperature

From the perspective of the lighting system designer, the correlated colour temperature (CCT) is the key feature in the selection of a light source since the CCT serves as an indicator of, not only the colour of the source, but also, the 'atmosphere' it will create.

The CCT is defined in [25], and its significance is that it describes the chromaticity of the source (which must be close to the Planckian locus) in the CIE (u, v) chromaticity diagram.[2] Note that it is possible for many different spectral power distributions (SPDs) to have the same CCT; and that CCT is not essentially linked with colour rendering, quality or fidelity.

---

[2] In CIE documentation, this is now replaced by the $(u', \frac{2}{3}v')$ diagram based on CIE 1976 (u', v') coordinates.

4. Optimisations

We here present, in outline form, the results of optimised spectral designs achieved using DE. Interested readers are referred to previous publications [23, 26–29] for full details.

It is noted at the outset that it is, in principle, possible to create white-light mixtures by the use of as few as two or three wavelengths. Our early experiments showed that these practically always lead to suboptimal mixtures in the sense that either one or both of LER and X_c are unacceptably low (X_c is here used to denote any one of the colour metrics mentioned in Section 3). Further experiments indicated that mixtures of five, six or seven wavelengths gave little or no practical advantage over 4-band mixtures, while adding to the complexity (and possible unreliability) of the light source. For the sake of brevity, therefore, the following descriptions are confined solely to results for 4-band mixing.

Two types of optimisation conditions are described: (i) constrained, in which the optimiser is presented with a set of known (e.g., commercial) monochromatic spectra, and is required to find the best available mixtures in terms of defined criteria and (ii) unconstrained, when the program is given mathematical descriptions for the shapes of potential monochromatic spectra, which it then proceeds to mix and optimise as above.

In the optimisations described below, all SPDs for LEDs were computed at 5-nm intervals, and for lasers at 1 nm.

4.1 Optimisation of LED mixtures for LER and CRI (CIE R_a)

This investigation [26] explored the optimisation of white-light mixtures of seven LEDs (four at a time) from the Lumileds Luxeon™ range [30] and it is therefore classed as constrained. The objective here was to achieve the best available combination of R_a with LER, and the fitness function for DE was defined as in Eq. 4:

$$f_{fit} = aR_a + bR_b + cR_c + d_{rad} + eR_{min} \tag{4}$$

where R_a = CIE general colour rendering index (based on 8 medium-chroma test colours); R_b = similar figure of merit based on the 6 additional test colours in the CIE method; R_c = similar figure of merit based on all 14 test colours in the CIE method; η_{rad} = the value of the LER (lumen per watt figure); R_{min} = the lowest value of R_i in the set of 14 individual values; a, b, c, d and e are user-selectable weights controlling the influence of R_a, R_b, R_c, η_{rad} and R_{min} on the optimisation process.

Experimentation found that f_{fit} converged around (or before) the 1000th generation; hence, the number of generations G was set to 1000 for fast and accurate convergence of the DE. Note that a too-small G can mean that the process has insufficient opportunity to search for effective solution vectors whereas, for excessive values of G, the optimisation process is unnecessarily slowed down without improving the optimisation result.

The other DE parameters that may influence the operation of the algorithm are P, F, and CR, all of which need to be set prior to any run. We found by experimentation that the values of these parameters had only a minor influence on the optimisation results; and the choice of suitable values for good optimisation was straightforward. We quickly settled on a value of P = 50, and we set F and CR according to the suggestions in [10], that is, F = 0.5 and CR = 0.1.

Further experimentation investigated the effects of different values for the weighting factors for f_{fit}, and some indicative results are shown in **Table 1**. The relative spectral power distribution (SPD) for the result listed as Test 1 is shown in **Figure 3**.

Test no	Weighting factors					Best results						
	a	*b*	*c*	*d*	*e*	R_a	R_b	R_c	η_{rad} (lm/W)	R_{min}	i_{min}	*CCT* (K)
1	1	1	1	1	10	95	96	91	339	76	12	3268
2	1	1	1	1	5	93	83	89	350	76	12	3074
3	1	1	1	0.5	0	92	79	87	384	58	9	3169

Table 1.
Influence of different f_{fit} weights on the optimization of LED mixtures.

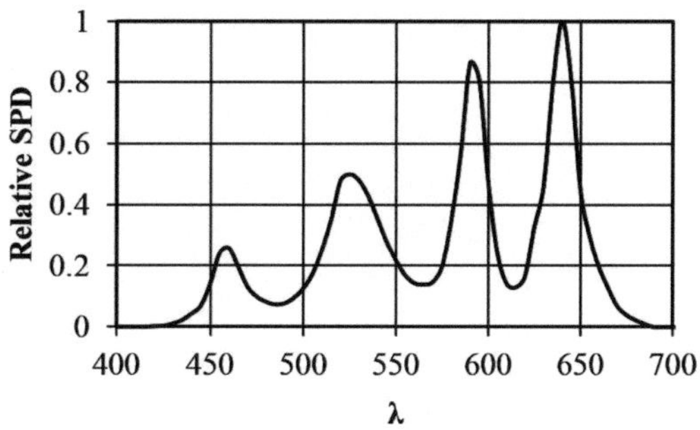

Figure 3.
Relative SPD of the 4-band LED mixture (Test 1). Wavelength peaks for: blue = 460 nm, green = 530 nm, amber = 590 nm, red = 630 nm. Source parameters: R_a = 95, R_b = 86, η_{rad} = 339 lm/W, CCT = 3268 K, R_{12} = 76 (blue sample).

It is worth noting that $R_a \geq 90$ is generally considered as excellent colour performance, and LER ≥ 300 lm/W exceeds that of many other (efficient) light sources.

Table 1 shows that significant step decrements in the weight *e* (the R_{min} weighting) led to fairly small losses in the colour performance of the mixtures, but to noticeable gains in LER (and hence, efficiency in use).

Figures 4 and **5** show how the individual elements of f_{fit} in Test 1 were fluctuating before converging to their final values.

It can be seen that η_{rad} (**Figure 5**), and hence also f_{fit}, undergoes significant swings during the early stages of the process ($G < 300$). It then converges to just below 340 lm/W at G = 336. In this instance, the population has converged around G = 400, and all parameters are only fine-tuned thereafter. These curves indicate that the process could, in fact, have been terminated at G = 500, with low likelihood of loss.

4.2 Optimisation of mathematical mixtures for LER and CRI (CIE R_a)

It was decided to extend the above approach to an unconstrained investigation of SPD mixtures defined by the following mathematical functions:

- Gaussian
- rectangular
- triangular

The optimiser was free to position four spectral bands, conforming to any one function, at any wavelength within the visible band (380–760 nm) and having any relative intensity (i.e., height) of one to another. One constraint was imposed for practical purposes, namely each band was kept to a spectral width between 25 and

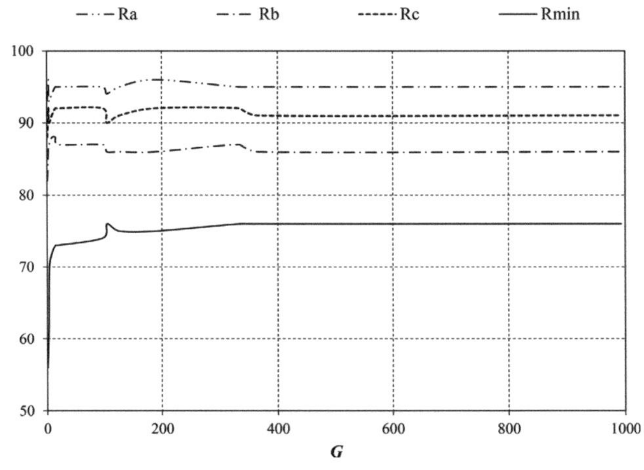

Figure 4.
Behaviour of R_a, R_b, R_c and R_{min} in Test 1.

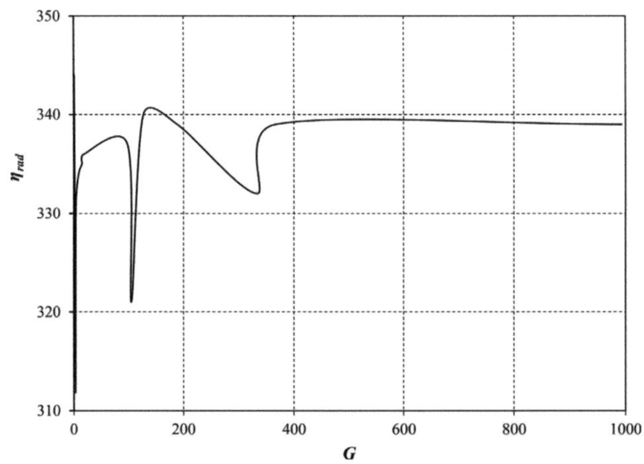

Figure 5.
Behaviour of η_{rad} in Test 1.

45 nm (full width at half maximum, or FWHM) [27]. Apart from these changes, the procedure was essentially the same as that used in Section 4.1, and the same fitness function was used.

A total of 36 optimisations were performed, using 12 different combinations of f_{fit} weightings for each of the three functions. The following extract from this set of results shows the SPDs obtained with the weightings: $a = 1$; $b = c = d = e = 0$. See **Figure 6**.

It was intended that the unconstrained approach will help to identify those wavelength combinations that will lead to optimum SPDs. The findings relating to the spectra in **Figure 6** are summarised in **Table 2**.

This is too small a sample from which to generalise; however, it is possible to make the following observations. The colour performance of these three mixtures is exceptionally good (other than the high CCT for G1) possibly at the expense of relatively moderate LER values. It is probable that the Gaussian and triangular shapes are more realistic simulations of real physical spectra (whether originating from LEDs or phosphors); hence their corresponding centre wavelengths (λ_1–λ_4) may be useful indicators for use in light-source design. See [27] for a more complete discussion.

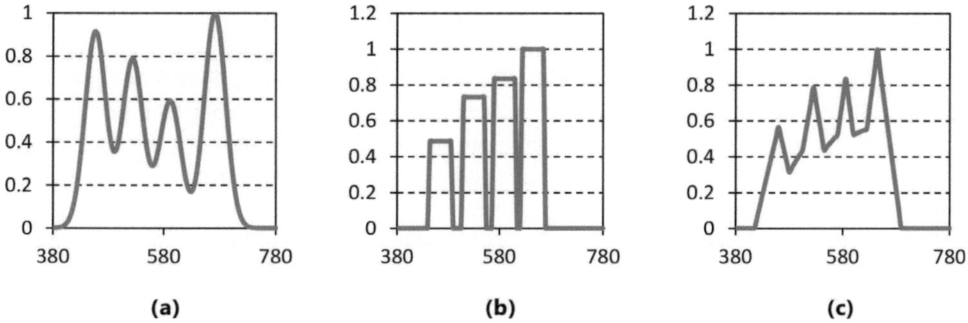

Figure 6.
Relative SPDs of the mathematical 4-band mixtures. (a) G1, Gaussian; (b) R1, rectangular; (c) T1, triangular f_{fit} = R_a.

Expt	R_a	R_b	R_c	η_R (lm/W)	R_{min}	i_{min}	T_C (K)	λ_1	λ_2	λ_3	λ_4
G1	98	93	96	228	80	12	7870	456	524	591	671
R1	97	90	94	317	72	12	3542	445	510	570	625
T1	98	95	97	303	84	12	4133	460	525	585	645

Table 2.
Results for the mixtures of mathematical functions shown in ***Figure 4****.*

4.3 Optimisation of LED mixtures for LER and CQS (NIST Q_a)

This was again a constrained optimisation process. It was based on the same set of Luxeon™ LEDs as used in Section 4.1, and also used tetrachromatic mixtures. The optimisation process [23] was also broadly similar to that in Section 4.1, and it used a similar interface, but the software was rewritten to compute the performance of candidate SPDs in terms of CQS parameters, specifically the average colour quality index, Q_a, and the minimum, Q_{min} (the lowest individual index, Q_i) for every candidate SPD.

The following fitness function (Eq. 5) was employed:

$$f_{fit} = aQ_a + b\eta_{rad} + cQ_{min} \tag{5}$$

where a, b, c are the weights controlling the influence of Q_a, LER and Q_{min} on the optimisation of the LED mixtures. A selection of the results of the optimisation of the LED mixtures using various weightings is shown in **Table 3**.

Weights			Optimised spectra			
a	b	c	Q_a	η_{rad} (lm/W)	Q_{min}	CCT (K)
1	0	0	96	306	93	3638
1	0	1	96	305	94	3386
0	0	1	96	298	94	3379
10	1	0	95	322	91	3452
0	1	2	84	367	75	5041

Table 3.
Optimizations of five tetrachromatic LED mixtures (CQS domain).

4.4 Optimisation of LED mixtures for specific CCT values

The previously mentioned techniques (used in Section 4.1–4.3) did not take account of the CCTs of the spectra except as values to be calculated following the optimisations. Because of the importance of the CCT to lighting designers and users, it was recognised that this parameter needed to be incorporated into the optimisation procedure.

We therefore designed a new optimisation tool [29], again based on differential evolution, which puts CCT at the centre of the process and then proceeds to optimise colour rendering while maintaining a close tolerance to the target CCT value. We selected three CCT values to illustrate the effectiveness of the process.

The optimiser was presented with a specific set of four monochromatic LED spectra selected from the Luxeon™ range. The objective was to minimise the average colour difference for a set of colour samples which, in principle, could be any suitable set of colours. We chose to use the 14 test colours specified in CIE13.3 [13] since they constitute a well-known and widely used set.

The basis of the selection process in our algorithm was the colour difference of specific surface colours as they appear under the candidate spectrum and under the reference spectrum of the same CCT. In each new generation, the offspring solutions were evaluated on the basis of minimising the colour difference $\Delta E_{00(Avg)}$ calculated using the CIEDE2000 colour difference formula [31]. Hence, the algorithm was designed to search for a spectrum with the lowest colour differences. The optimum solution was determined after having performed *G* generations (typically 1000); that is, the best solution in generation *G* is accepted as the best white-light spectrum.

Figure 7 shows the results in the form of the SPDs realised by the LED mixtures, and their performance is summarised in **Table 4**. Note that $\Delta E_{00(Avg)}$ represents the average of 14 colour differences (for the 14 colours in the CIE set) and $\Delta(u',v')$ is the chromaticity difference in CIE 1976 coordinates between the target CCT and that achieved by the LED mixture. The other listed parameters were computed after the completion of each optimisation run.

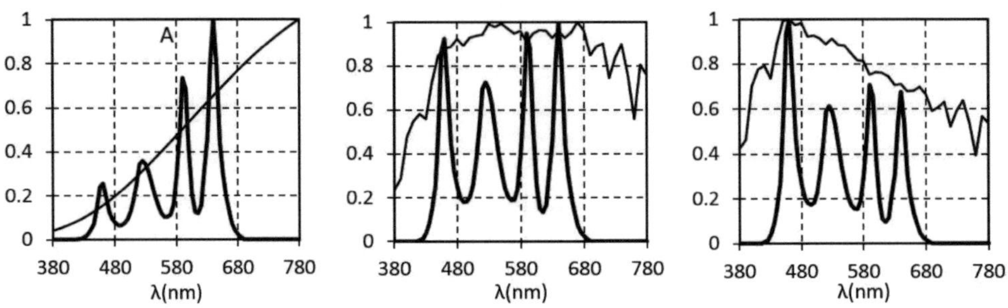

Figure 7.
Relative SPDs of 4-LED mixtures that match CIE illuminants A, D50 and D65. Relative SPDs of the actual illuminants are shown for reference (lighter lines).

Illuminant	R_a	R_{min}	i_{min}	LER (lm/W)	$\Delta E_{00(Avg)}$	$\Delta(u',v')$
A	93	68	11	313	0.73	0.0038
D50	95	70	12	311	0.81	0.0010
D65	95	63	12	298	0.94	0.0015

Table 4.
Optimizations of tetrachromatic LED mixtures with specified CCTs.

Illuminant	R_a	R_{min}	i_{min}	LER (lm/W)	$\Delta E_{00(Avg)}$	$\Delta(u',v')$
A	96	68	12	318	0.82	0.0034
D50	95	89	12	336	0.58	0.0019
D65	93	75	9	299	0.67	0.0059

Table 5.
Optimizations of tetrachromatic Gaussian mixtures with specified CCTs.

The above approach was extended to a set of optimisations in which Gaussian-shaped spectra of either 25 or 50 nm bandwidth, but with unconstrained peak intensities and wavelengths, were optimised in the same way as the LED mixtures.

Table 5 shows the best CRI performance for 4-band (25 nm) Gaussian mixtures, along with the other properties as listed in **Table 4**, and there is an evident degree of conformance between the two sets of results.

4.5 Optimisation of laser diode mixtures using TM-30-15 (IES R_f)

Our investigations in this field [28, 32] were inspired by the work of Neumann et al. [33] who successfully demonstrated a white-light 4-laser mixture with acceptable colour properties expressed in terms of the CRI and CQS metrics. Our earlier paper [28] also used CRI and CQS as measures of colour rendition. These approaches are now regarded as suspect (particularly in respect of mixtures of ultra-narrow bands such as lasers) on the grounds of incomplete sampling of wavelength and colour spaces.

Our purpose in [32] was to optimise similar mixtures of solid-state lasers, and to utilize the more up-to-date method of the IES colour fidelity index R_f [15, 16].

A new optimisation tool was designed to implement the complex sequence of non-linear calculation steps in the evaluation of colour fidelity for any given SPD. We then developed a new fitness function (Eq. 6) based on the IES parameters as well as the LER, to evaluate every candidate spectrum produced in the process.

$$f = aR_f + bR_{f\ \min} + cR_{f\ \text{skin}} + d\eta_{rad} \qquad (6)$$

where R_f = average fidelity index for all 99 colour samples; R_{fmin} = value of the lowest-scoring individual R_f (single colour sample); R_{fskin} = average index for two individual colours selected as representative of human skin; η_{rad} = value of LER in lm/W; a, b, c, d are the respective weighting factors.

For the purposes of optimisation, each laser was simulated by a pseudo-delta function (1-nm bandwidth) at the centre wavelength of its output. Optimisations were performed in both constrained (using commercially available laser diode wavelengths) and unconstrained modes.

The best result (with four real laser wavelengths) was R_f of 84 with LER 364 lm/W, which indicates the feasibility of the mixed-laser approach to provide highly efficient, energy-saving light sources. The unconstrained mixtures showed that the prospects will be further enhanced by potential future developments in semiconductor lasers, with the possibility of producing R_f of 86 with LER of 380 lm/W. The detailed properties for these two mixtures are given in **Table 6**.

Compared with LEDs, lasers have the advantage of higher conversion efficiency (from electrical input to radiant output). This, combined with the very high prospective LER values, will make future laser mixtures exceptionally attractive in terms of energy conservation. The colour properties are not as good as for LEDs, but they are nevertheless regarded as sufficiently good for many types of lighting

Simulation mode	R_f	$R_{f\ skin}$	$R_{f\ min}$	i_{min}	LER (lm/W)	CCT (K)
Constrained	84	87	59	97	364	3011
Unconstrained	86	91	54	81	380	3156

i_{min} refers to the sample number that gave the listed value of $R_{f\ i} = R_{f\ min}$.
i = 97 is dark pink-purple (printed origin); 81 is dark purple-blue (natural origin).

Table 6.
Optimizations of simulated tetrachromatic laser mixtures.

situations. Lasers are not yet considered to be practical as white-light sources but, with the potential for new developments in solid-state visible laser sources, their future prospects must be very strong.

5. Conclusions

We have here demonstrated the power of the differential evolution algorithm in the intelligent design of light source spectra, based on both LEDs and laser diodes. It provides a simple, flexible and effective solution in the elusive search for the balance of the LER and the colour rendition properties in optimised light sources. We recommend this technique to anyone engaged in the optimum design of light-source spectra.

We feel confident that our method can also be readily adapted to other types of optimisation problem, wherever suitable elements for the fitness function can be readily identified.

Acknowledgements

This work was supported by Professional Engineering and the Manukau Institute of Technology Research Fund. The second author thanks Professor Ahmed Al-Jumaily, director of IBTec at AUT, for his support and the provision of facilities.

Conflicts of interest

The authors declare that there is no conflict of interest regarding the publication of this chapter.

Funding statement

This study has been supported in part by a Manukau Institute of Technology Research Grant, and was also performed as part of the employment of the authors by Manukau Institute of Technology.

Data availability

Previously reported data were used to support this study. These prior studies are cited at relevant places within the text as references [23, 26–29, 32].

Author details

Snjezana Soltic[1]* and Andrew N. Chalmers[2]

1 Manukau Institute of Technology, Auckland, New Zealand

2 Institute of Biomedical Technologies, Auckland University of Technology, Auckland, New Zealand

*Address all correspondence to: ssoltic@manukau.ac.nz

References

[1] Lei Z, Xia G, Ting L, Xiaoling G, Ming LQ, Guangdi S. Color rendering and luminous efficacy of trichromatic and tetrachromatic LED-based white LEDs. Microelectronics Journal. 2007; **38**:1-6

[2] Stevenson R. The LED's dark secret. IEEE Spectrum. August 2009:23-27

[3] Bergh A, Craford G, Duggal A, Haitz R. The promise and challenge of solid-state lighting. Physics Today. 2001; **54**(12):42-47

[4] Ohno Y. Simulation analysis of white LED spectra and color rendering. CIE Expert Symposium on LED Light Sources, Tokyo; 2004

[5] Žakauskas A, Vaicekauskas R, Ivanauskas F, Gaska R, Shur S. Optimization of white polychromatic semiconductor lamps. Applied Physics Letters. 2002;**80**(2):234-236

[6] Protzman JB, Houser KW. LEDs for general illumination: The state of the science. Leucos. 2006;**3**(2):121-142

[7] Chalmers AN, Cuttle C, Wang L, Luong P. The quest for high-rendering high-luminous-efficacy light sources. In: IESANZ Convention; Queenstown, New Zealand. 2008

[8] Lu Y, Gao Y, Chen H, Chen Z. Intelligent spectra design and colorimetric parameter analysis for light-emitting diodes. In: 14th International Conference on Mechatronics and Machine Vision in Practice, M2VIP 2007, 4-6 Dec. 2007. pp. 118-122

[9] Storn R, Price K. Differential evolution: A simple and efficient adaptive scheme for global optimization over continuous spaces. In: Technical Report TR-95-012. Berkley: International Computer Science Institute; 1995

[10] Storn R, Price K. Differential evolution: A simple and efficient heuristic for global optimization over continuous space. Journal of Global Optimization. 1997;**11**:341-359

[11] Karaboğa D, Ökdem S. A simple and global optimization algorithm for engineering problems: Differential evolution algorithm. Turkey Journal of Electrical Engineering. 2004;**12**(1): 53-60

[12] Vesterstrøm J, Thomsen R. A comparative study of differential evolution, particle swarm optimization, and evolutionary algorithms on numerical bench problems. In: Congress on Evolutionary Computation, 19–23 June; vol. 2. 2004. pp. 1980-1987

[13] CIE. Method of Measuring and Specifying Colour Rendering Properties of Light Sources. Vienna: CIE Publication 13.3, CIE; 1995

[14] Fumagalli S, Bonanomi C, Rizzi A. Experimental assessment of color-rendering indices and color appearance under varying setups. Journal of Modern Optics. 2015;**62**(1):56-66

[15] Illuminating Engineering Society of North America. IES Method for Evaluating Light Source Color Rendition. New York: Illuminating Engineering Society; 2015

[16] David A, Fini PT, Houser KW, Ohno Y, Royer MP, Smet KAG, et al. Development of the IES method for evaluating the color rendition of light sources. Optics Express. 2015;**23**(12): 15888-15906

[17] Royer MP, Wei M. The role of presented objects in deriving color

preference criteria from psychophysical studies. LEUKOS. 2017;**13**(3):143-157

[18] Smet KAG, David A, Whitehead L. Why color space uniformity and sample set spectral uniformity are essential for color rendering measures. LEUKOS. 2016;**12**(1–2):39-50

[19] Luo MR, Cui G, Li C. Uniform colour spaces based on CIECAM02 colour appearance model. Color Research and Application. 2006;**31**: 320-330

[20] CIE. A Colour Appearance Model for Colour Management Systems: CIECAM02. Vienna: CIE Publication 159, CIE; 2004

[21] Davis W, Ohno Y. Color quality scale. Optical Engineering. 2010;**49**(3): 033602

[22] Fairchild MD. Color Appearance Models. 3rd ed. New York: Wiley; 2013

[23] Soltic S, Chalmers AN. Differential evolution for the optimisation of multi-band white LED light sources. Lighting Research and Technology. 2012;**44**(2): 224-237

[24] Wyszecki G, Stiles WS. Color Science: Concepts and Methods, Quantitative Data and Formulae. 2nd ed. New York: Wiley; 1982

[25] Commission Internationale de l'Eclairage. Colorimetry. 3rd ed. Vienna: CIE Publication 15.3, CIE; 2003

[26] Soltic S, Chalmers AN. Differential evolution and its application to intelligent spectral design. In: Proceedings of the 16th Electronics New Zealand Conference (ENZCon); Dunedin: University of Otago. 2009

[27] Chalmers AN, Soltic S. Light source optimization: Spectral design and simulation of four-band white-light sources. Optical Engineering. 2012; **51**(4):044003

[28] Soltic S, Chalmers AN. Optimization of laser-based white light illuminants. Optics Express. 2013;**21**(7):8964-8971

[29] Soltic S, Chalmers AN. Optimization of multiband white-light illuminants for specified color temperatures. Advances in OptoElectronics. 2015. DOI: 10.1155/ 2015/263791. Article ID: 263791

[30] Lighting L. Luxeon® K2 Emitter, Technical Datasheet DS51. San Jose, California: Lumileds Lighting US LLC; 2006

[31] CIE. Improvement to Industrial Colour-difference Evaluation. Vienna: CIE Publication. 142, CIE; 2001

[32] Soltic S, Chalmers AN. Prospects for 4-Laser white-light sources. Journal of Modern Optics. 2018;**66**(3):271-280. DOI: 10.1080/09500340.2018.1517904

[33] Neumann A, Wierer JJ Jr, Davis W, Ohno Y, Brueck SRJ, Tsao JY. Four-color laser white illuminant demonstrating high color-rendering quality. Optics Express. 2011;**19**(S4 Suppl 4):A982-A990

Chapter 5

Interpreting Analysis on Rhetorical Strategies Modeling in Computer Science Research Articles

Ina Suryani, Mohd Mustafa Al Bakri Abdullah and Hazry Desa

Abstract

Description on rhetorical strategies modeling proposed by experts in the field of language provides clues on strategies used in research writing. However, the interpretation and analysis on the utilization of the rhetorical strategies models are limited to comparing the strategies used in articles grouped according to research disciplines such as biomedical, linguistics, and arts. In view of the constraint, this chapter focuses on the interpretations of rhetorical strategies modeling by analyzing the computer science research articles in a few categories. The first interpretation of analysis is on the articles with high and low citation index, followed by analysis on the articles grouped according to journal wise population and lastly analysis on articles written by non-native writers. The interpretation of the analysis suggested that the strategies proposed in the models are used differently by the writers of articles with high and low citations, writers of different journals, and non-native writers. The descriptions provided in this chapter account on the important strategies utilized by highly cited writers, specific journals, and non-native writers.

Keywords: technical writing, rhetorical strategies, research article, writing, computer science, text analytics

1. Introduction

In tandem to the dire need to increase the quantity and quality of research article publication, easier ways to write research articles are studied globally on a large scale [1–4]. Some of the studies have derived models that simplify the strategies for writing, for example, Swales' CARS models [5–7] which are examples of prominent models that are being used among many research writers. The models are based on an earlier model that was derived from "an analysis of 158 research article introductions in English distributed across various discipline areas" ([8], p. 241). Descriptions on rhetorical strategies modeling proposed by experts in the field of language provide clues on strategies used in research writing such as the Four-move models for research article introductions [5], CARS model [6, 7], Multiperspective Model [9], Project Justifying Model [10], and Problem Justifying Model [11]. These models have been utilized by writers to write better. Ahmad [10] did an initial

IntechOpen

analysis for Malay scientific research articles, and from here, she proposed the Project-justifying model. Safnil [11] came up with a new model Problem Justifying Project (PJP) for rhetorical analysis on Indonesian research article introductions. This chapter describes the strategies used in research articles by presenting the analysis using the model.

Following the models over the years, researches have progressed in having the models tested and extended [12, 13]. Adnan [12] used Bunton's model, which was also a modification of Swales' model [6], to study the introductory sections of PhD theses and proposed some extension on the model. Adnan [12] analyzed the Indonesian research article introductions in education discipline and also proposed some extension after finding none of the research articles' introductions fit the CARS model and only less than half fit the Problem Justifying Project (PJP) model proposed by Safnil [11]. Briefly, while the major models [5–7, 10, 11] provide valuable guidelines on how writers write their research, further studies on the models showed that the applications of the strategies suggested in the model are applied differently across the discipline. The strategies suggested by the models are more prominent or less preferred in different disciplines. Accordingly, this chapter focuses the analysis on research article in computer science discipline.

The interpretation and analysis on the utilization of the rhetorical strategies models are mostly on comparing the strategies used in articles grouped according to research disciplines such as biomedical [14] linguistics and arts. Many have reported on such analysis on computer science research article [15, 16]. In view of extending the study in this area, this chapter focuses the interpretations of rhetorical strategies modeling by analyzing the articles in a few categories. The first interpretation of analysis is on the articles with high and low citation index, followed by analysis on the articles grouped according to journal-wise population and lastly analysis on articles written by non-native writers [14, 17, 18].

2. Rhetorical models for research articles

Some models used in other research article genre studies are Four-move model [5], CARS model [6–8], Project Justifying Model [10], Problem solution model [19], Problem Justifying Project model [11], and Ideal problem solution model [12]. Critiques on problem-focused models pointed out that not all research begin with a problem or "have a recognizable problem" and the other models [10–12] are for research article introductions in other languages than English. Bhatia ([9], p. 11) commended the Swales model as capable to "introduce a thick description of language in use" apart from "Combine socio-cultural" and "Psycholinguistic (including cognitive) aspects of text construction and interpretation with linguistic insights." This study chooses the model by Swales [7] to be used.

CARS model [7] also begins with establishing a territory and topic generalization. However, in this revised model, citations are required and the topic generalization has the quality of increasing specificity to the intended research. The review of previous research is deemed as an obligatory support for the steps on establishing territory and topic generalization with increasing specificity. There are a few reasons as to why this study uses the CARS model version 2004. The reasons are mainly concerned with the dynamic nature of the research article [7, 20] problems pointed out by previous researchers in using the 1990 model [7, 20], and the improvements made in the 2004 version by Swales himself [7].

The next move suggested in the model is Move 2, which establishes a research niche. In this move, the writer reveals the niche or the specialized area in the subject which has already been mentioned in general, earlier in Move 1. The writers may support this move with citations. This move is further realized either by indicating a gap or by adding more information to what is known. "Adding to what is known" is a strategy where the previous research is reviewed, development in the research area is explained, unresolved matters in the research are pointed out and the stance on the research development is presented.

After fulfilling either of these two steps, Swales [7] added that writers may repeat the previous moves and this recycling step is with increasing specificity toward the intended research. This move is dependent on the other moves mentioned before because it is actually a repetition of Move 1 and Move 2. The next step in Move 2 is presenting justification where the writer, one way or the other, asserts that the research must be carried on. However, this step is optional so the writer may or may not present the justification for the intended study.

Move 3 in the CARS model is about presenting the present work, which is a strategy that is gaining more importance particularly when the number of publication escalates every year and the competition among the submissions to the editorial also intensifies. The strategy on presenting the present work may affect how the research article fares against other submissions. In facing the competition, the presentation of the research work in the introduction must be interesting, relevant, worthy, and is able to captivate the intended audience.

Swales [7] suggested seven steps on accomplishing Move 3. Out of the steps listed, one step is obligatory step, three are optional steps, and three other steps are probable in some fields, but unlikely in others. Step 1 in Move 3 is the obligatory step, which is announcing the present research descriptively and/or purposively [7]. In this obligatory step, the readers are presented with the information on what the rest of the paper is going to be reporting or discussing. The model puts it that this can be done in two ways: purposively, which is by stating the purpose and reasons on why the study is done and/or descriptively, which is by describing, listing, and recounting the composition of the study. Shehzad ([20] p. 139) elaborated that purposive announcement is where the authors indicate their main purpose or purposes or outline the "nature of the study", and descriptive announcement is where the authors "describe the main feature of their research." In other words, this step is where the readers are informed about the reasons, and the rationale of the study is presented.

The next step for Move 3 is Step 2, which states the research questions or hypothesis and is suggested as an optional step. Presenting the present research is described the step being utilized by native writers as being "more explicit about what the researchers are investigating, an approach that makes their text less demanding to the reader" (**Figure 1**, [21], p. 246).

The following step for Move 3 is definitional clarifications that can be realized by giving brief explanations on some of the methods, terms, techniques, modes, or concepts related to the study. This step is optional and the reason for having the definitional clarification is to give a clear meaning to the item in context and regularize it. Another optional step for Move 3 is summarizing methods where brief information on the method used in the study is presented. Steps 2–4 are not only optional but also less fixed in order.

The following steps of 5–7 are probable in some fields but unlikely in others. Step 5 is announcing principle outcome where the main findings of the study are presented to establish the research contribution as early as possible in the research article. While Swales [6] listed this step as probable in some fields, studies on computer science research articles have shown that this step is obligatory among the computer science writers [15, 22, 23]. The next step is Step 6 that states the value of the present research. This step is also reported as obligatory in the computer science research article introductions [16, 24]. In this step, the writers promote their

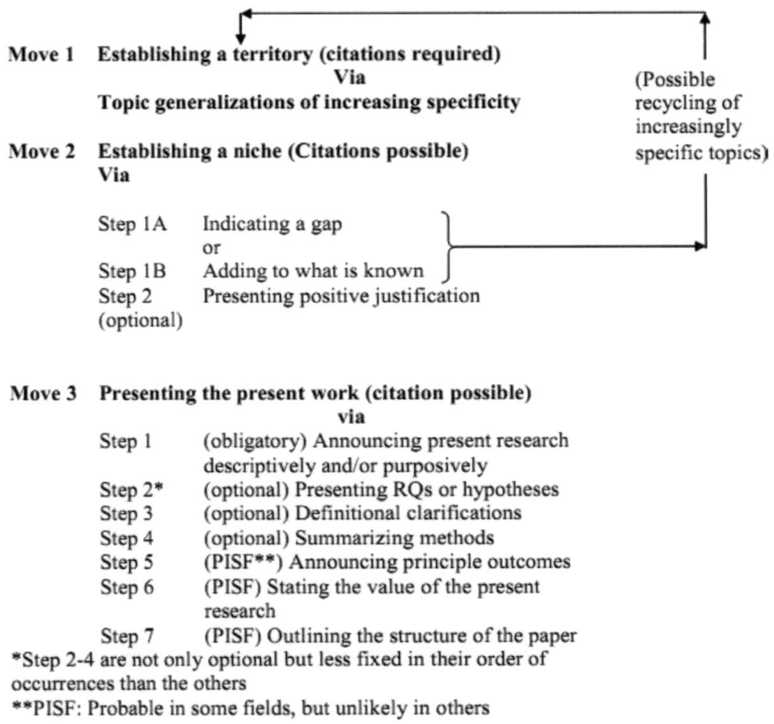

Figure 1.
CARS model version 2004 [6].

studies and highlight the value of their research. The last step in the CARS model [7] is outlining the structure of the paper where the outline of the research article is briefly explained.

3. Method and instrument

The study uses qualitative method and the approach is top-down. Qualitative method with top-down approach calls for emphasis on meaning and ideas rather that the language structure and lexical formation. The analysis focuses on the discourse structure in the text written in the area of the targeted discipline. In this analysis, "moves" in the text is identified in series of sequences. Every "move" is identified to the communicative function. The examination on the moves starts with the establishment of an analytical framework. And then, the moves types are identified and described.

It started with choosing 120 research articles. About 150 articles were chosen because the data gathered from the articles have reached saturation. The next step was to conduct the move analysis on the research articles. This study wanted to know what were the moves and steps being used in the articles.

3.1 The corpus

The corpus of the study consisted of the computer science research articles written by academicians in Malaysian Universities, which were listed in Scopus in the year 2010. The Malaysian Universities Computer Science Scopus Articles Corpus was created for this study and included 150 computer science research articles written by academicians in Malaysian universities. Analysis on the introduction sections was conducted, which comprised 98,597 words.

The list of the intended journals was generated from the SciVerse Scopus database using the following steps. First, the list of private and public universities was obtained from the Ministry of Higher Education Website. The Ministry of Higher Education Website listed 20 public universities and 25 private universities [25]. Next, the number of Scopus publications by each of the 45 universities was retrieved from the Scopus database system. This information was obtained using the affiliation search function and the spellings used on the Ministry of Higher Education Website.

Since the number of publications consisted of various documents such as articles, conference papers, reviews, articles, short summaries, conference reviews, editorial reviews, and even notes, the search was narrowed down further to research articles only. But the number obtained included the number of articles in various fields. As this study focused on computer science, the search was narrowed down to computer science. The next step involved excluding articles in multidisciplinary areas because such inclusion also included articles other than those in the computer science discipline.

A total of 150 articles were chosen because the data gathered from the articles have reached saturation. Patton [26] stated that sample size can be affected by "the purpose of the inquiry" which in this study refers to "identify patterns across data." This study wanted to know what the moves are and steps being used in the articles and how the moves and steps were realized. As suggested by Shehzad [27], the articles were selected and added. Initially, the analysis of the articles indicated some patterns that lead to categories of how the moves and steps were realized. More articles were added until the analysis showed that new articles no longer generate new patterns and categories on how the moves and steps were realized. After analyzing 120 articles, the patterns on how the moves and steps were realized became regular and predictable. For example, in the analysis of Move 2 Step 1A, four categories were identified; after adding more articles up to 150, the categories became consistent and no new categories emerged because the patterns can just fit into the existing for categories. Similar consistency was noted in the categories for the other moves and steps upon reaching 150 articles. The data has reached saturation at 150 articles and no pattern or category emerged from addition of article, and therefore, the size of the corpus consists of 150 articles.

Shehzad [27] suggests that a corpus should be authentic and follow specific criteria and should be taken from high ranking journals as the high rank reflects the publication's soundness [28]. On the same note, the research articles in this study were taken from the Scopus indexed database. If the study uses articles from non-Scopus database, the samples derived from the non-Scopus articles may not be suitable for learners who aim to publish in the Scopus indexed journal.

The 2010 publication was chosen because as the database was already completed, the citation index had grown substantially and had become more constant in terms of citing hierarchy. The citation index is an important criterion for this study because of a few reasons. For one reason, citation index is systematically generated to indicate the number of times the paper has been cited by other writers. As such, it is more neutral and unprejudiced in determining the value of the research articles. Moreover, citation index for publications is also one of the sought-after criteria for university ranking in Malaysia [29, 30]. As such, citation index has been taken into account in the performance evaluation of the academicians [29, 31]. Given its importance, citation was also included as a criterion of selection for the corpus.

3.2 Sampling on high and low citation groups

For the analysis of the data, the citations of the research article were also considered. Research articles with six citations or more were grouped together in the research articles with more citation group. Research articles with zero citation were grouped in the research articles with lesser citation group.

Research articles with citation of one to five were not included in any group and were not counted in this analysis. The reason was to give the two groups the difference in citations which was needed to achieve the purpose of the analysis. It is noteworthy that the analysis was meant to obtain the description on the moves and steps that have been used in the higher citation research articles. The moves and steps of the research articles with lower citations are also noted and analyzed. Consequently, if the difference of citations between the two groups is only by one citation, the findings on the moves and steps may not show much difference and actually may also be similar descriptions. The elimination of research articles with citations of one to five, there would be a difference of six citations between the groups. A bigger difference established between the two groups is needed to ensure that the two groups are really distinct and the research articles are not in either group by chance. High citation groups consist of 62 research articles, while research articles with lesser citation groups have 65 research articles. For the analysis, the total moves and steps for each group was turned into percentages and comparisons were made in terms of the moves and steps accomplished.

3.3 Sampling on journal wise group

In journal wise sampling, the research articles are taken from a selection of journals instead of random journals for the reason that research articles from the same journals showed more cohesive findings. Studies [15, 16] have shown that more regular patterns were detected in research articles from the same journal.

Two Malaysian journals, the Malaysian Journal of Computer Science and PERTANIKA Science and Technology, were chosen. All articles published in the journal for 2010 were included. The Malaysian Journal of Computer Sciences is published by the Faculty of Computer Science and Information Technology, University of Malaya. The journal has been in circulation since 1985 and is indexed in Scopus since 2007 and is also abstracted in ISI and a few other databases [32, 34].

The journal publications also include research articles from local and foreign universities, not limited to the academics only but also consisting of the works from the business and industrial sectors in the field of Computer Science and Information Technology. Pertanika Journal of Science and Technology is published by Universiti Putra Malaysia. The area for the research articles in this publication includes a wider scope than those in the Malaysian Journal of Computer Science. Apart from Computer Science and Information Technology, it also covers research in the area of bioinformatics, bioscience, biotechnology, and bio-molecular sciences,

4. Results and discussion

The results of the study are presented according to the groupings in the following sections.

4.1 Results on high and low citation index

The analysis according to the citation index shows that the highly cited research article accomplished more of the moves and steps recommended in CARS model [6] compared to the research articles that have never been cited. First, the analysis showed that research articles with high citation have a higher percentage of realizations in presenting the present work. Ninety-seven percent of the highly cited articles accomplished this strategy, while only 83% of research articles with zero citation utilized this move, thereby suggesting that more highly cited writer utilized this strategy compared to the writers with zero or less citation.

Second, the difference in percentage between the two groups in realizing this move is also found in the use of announcing the present research descriptively. Compared with the research articles with zero citation, the highly cited research articles were more inclined to fulfill this step at 92%, which indicate that the step has been used at obligatory level, just as suggested in the CARS model [6]. On the other hand, only 75% of the research articles with zero citation use this strategy.

Finally, the findings also shows that apart from these two differences, the highly cited research articles were also more inclined to utilize the strategy proposed in the Swales [6] model of Move 3 compared to the research articles that had never been cited. **Table 1** shows the summary on moves and steps by high and low citation groups.

Apart from the two steps explained in this paragraph, compared to the research articles that had never been cited, highly cited research articles are also more inclined to utilize the strategy proposed in the Swales [6] model in Move 3.

Moves and steps		Percentages High citation	Percentages Low citation
Move 1	Establishing a territory Topic generalizations of increasing specificity	97	91
Move 2	Establishing a niche (citations possible)	100	100
	Step 1A: indicating a gap	86	71
	Step IB: adding to what is known	100	100
	Step 2: presenting positive justifications (optional)	68	52
Move 3	Presenting the present work	97	83
	Step 1 (obligatory): announcing present research descriptively and/or purposively	92	75
	Step 2 (optional): presenting the hypothesis or the research question	0	1
	Step 3 (optional): giving clarification on the definitions	18	20
	Step 4 (optional): giving brief information about the methods used	55	40
	Step 5 (PISF): informing the readers about the principle outcomes	14	12
	Step 6 (PISF): informing the readers about the value of the research in context	44	28
	Step 7 (PISF): giving an overview on the structure of the research article	36	20

Table 1.
Summary on moves and steps by high and low citation groups.

In summary, the highly cited research article group has better accomplishment in presenting the summary of the methods in the Introduction section. The interesting finding is in the step of Move 3 Step 6 "Stating the value of the present research." The analysis shows that 44% of the research articles with high citation utilized this strategy. On the other hand, only 28% of the zero cited research articles accomplished this strategy. The big difference in percentage between the two groups for this step is more noticeable and evident. This big difference suggested and marked that authors of research articles with high citation count were more adamant and persistent in announcing the findings of their study and promoting the value of their research work. Such promotion and statement provides the readers with anticipation on the value and relevance of the articles, hence may increase readership which in turn increase the chance for citation. The research articles with low citation count did not perform this strategy as well as the other group. The percentage on the practice is lower. Despite the fact that the authors of this group stated the findings and the values of their study, the announcement on these matters were postponed and were written in the later section. Many of the authors in this group wrote the findings and values of their research in the "Findings and Discussion" section. The section is toward the end of the article and would have required the readers to reader longer. Move 3 Step 7, "Outlining the structure of the paper," suggested by CARS model [6] is the last strategy proposed. In presenting the research work, this step was also "probable in some fields, but unlikely in others." The findings show that 36% of the research articles with high citation count practiced this strategy successfully. Then, again only 20% of the zero cited research articles accomplished this strategy. The analysis of the findings suggested that the research articles with high citation count were more insistent and bold in presenting the research work. The research articles with high citation counts not only tell the readers about the structure of the paper but also revealed briefly the overview of the following sections. By writing this in the Introduction section, the readers can anticipate what the research article is about and how relevant the rest of the article is. In addition, the readers can also skip directly to the intended part for reading.

The study shows that the highly cited research articles utilize more strategies proposed in the Swales [6] model compared to the research articles that had never been cited. The findings also stressed the need for writers to be more assertive in promoting their research work in the introduction paragraph by utilizing the "Announcing the principle outcome" and "stating the value of the present research" steps.

4.2 Results on journal-wise population

The finding for Move 3 also confirmed that journal selection influences the way rhetorical structure is realized in the research articles. **Table 2** summarizes that both journals do have a similar structure to the general computer science research article structure found in the studies using global writers' work [14, 15, 22, 24, 33]. However, the obligatory and optional status of the moves and steps differed for Pertanika Journal. The research articles from the Pertanika Journal did not emphasis on presenting their present work in the Introduction section.

Rather, the presentation of their research work is delayed in the next section. Such preference is explained by reading the articles further, which shows that this journal has Materials and Method section after the Introduction section. Most writers began to introduce the intended study in Materials and Method section instead of doing so in the Introduction section.

Most of the research articles in the Malaysian Journal of Computer Science, on the other hand, followed the contemporary Introduction-Method-Result-Discussion

Moves and steps		Percentages for Pertanika	Percentages for MJCS
Move 1	Establishing a territory Topic generalizations of increasing specificity	95	100
Move 2	Establishing a niche (citations possible)	95	100
	Step 1A: indicating a gap	71	78
	Step IB: adding to what is known	97	93
	Step 2: presenting positive justifications (optional)	53	78
Move 3	Presenting the present work	79	100
	Step 1 (obligatory): announcing present research descriptively and/or purposively	76	100
	Step 2 (optional): presenting the hypothesis or the research question	0	0
	Step 3 (optional): giving clarification on the definitions	18	14
	Step 4 (optional): giving brief information about the methods used	39	21
	Step 5 (PISF): informing the readers about the principle outcomes	10	28
	Step 6 (PISF): informing the readers about the value of the research in context	26	57
	Step 7 (PISF): giving an overview on the structure of the research article	8	57

Table 2.
Move and steps by journal-wise population.

sections structure. As such, the presentations of the intended research are mostly done in the Introduction section.

However, it is important to note that the promotional steps in both journals are low compared to the findings in the studies using global writers' work [14, 22, 24, 25, 33]. The percentages for the promotional moves are below 80%. Announcing principle outcomes is scored at only 10% in Pertanika journal and only 28% in Malaysian Journal of Computer Science. The other step related to promotional strategy is stating the value of the present research, which is realized at 26% in Pertanika journal and 57% in Malaysian Journal of Computer Science. It can be concluded that the promotional strategies in the research articles of both journals can be further enhanced by using these two steps.

Findings on M3S5 by the university group percentage of announcing principle outcome. Similarly, analyzing the corpus based on the journal-wise population, the research articles from Malaysian Journal of Computer Science used this step more frequently compared to the research articles in the Pertanika journal. Twenty-eight percent of the research articles in Malaysian Journal of Computer Science utilized this step, whereas only 10% of the research articles in the Pertanika journal accomplish this step in the Introduction section.

The analysis for this group also shows that the research articles in the Malaysian Journal of Computer Science are more prone to presenting the present research work via outlining the structure of the paper compared to the research articles in the Pertanika journal. Fifty-seven percent of the research articles in the Malaysian

Journal of Computer Science employed this step, whereas only 8% of the research articles in the Pertanika Journal utilized this move.

All in all, the findings indicate that the utilization of the strategies differs from journal to journal; therefore, writers must understand the preference of the journal and tailor their writing to the style of the targeted journal.

4.3 Results on non-native writers

In this analysis, the findings of the study that is focused on non-native writers are compared to the findings in the study by Shehzad [24] who analyzed the strategies in Swales model among the global writers.

Table 3 shows that 94% of the article introduction sections in the study utilized Move 1 at an obligatory level, which is close to the 95% occurrences in the study by Shehzad [24]. Similarly, the strategy of establishing the research niche has also been fulfilled by all writers in this study. However, the strategy of indicating a gap has been underutilized by only 73% of the writers as compared to 95% accomplishment in the study by Shehzad [24] and 91.7% in a similar study by Anthony [33]. The strategy of Move 2 Step 1A which is "Indicating a gap" is underutilized. Studies on global writers [24, 33] have reported that this step is used at an obligatory level by the computer science writers; therefore, the awareness on the potential of this strategy among the non-native writers must be asserted so that the non-native writers would utilize this strategy more frequently.

On the other hand, 99% of the non-native writers in this study are more fond of using Move 2 Step 1B which is "Adding to what is known." However, this step

	This study	Shehzad [24]
Move 1 Establishing a territory Topic generalizations of increasing specificity	94%—obligatory	95%— obligatory
Move 2 Establishing a niche (citations possible)	100%—obligatory	93%— obligatory
Step 1A: indicating a gap	73%—optional (underutilized)	95%— obligatory
Step IB: adding to what is known	99%—obligatory	NA
Step 2: presenting positive justifications (optional)	62%—optional	NA
Move 3 Presenting the present work	91%—obligatory	NA
Step 1 (obligatory): announcing present research descriptively and/or purposively	86%—optional (underutilized)	98%— obligatory
Step 2 (optional): presenting RQ or hypothesis	1%—optional	32%—optional
Step 3 (optional): definitional clarifications	17%—optional	NA
Step 4 (optional): summarizing methods	53%—optional	NA
Step 5 (PISF): announcing principle outcomes	15%—optional (underutilized)	73%— obligatory
Step 6 (PISF): stating the value of the present research	35%—optional (underutilized)	55%— obligatory
Step 7 (PISF): outlining the structure of the paper	34%—optional (underutilized)	86%— obligatory

Table 3.
Results on non-native writers.

is not available in the previous CARS model [5], which is used by Shehzad [24]; so, it is not possible to compare the practice with the global writers. Move 2 Step 2 "Presenting positive justifications" is also not reported by Shehzad [24] and only occurred in 62% of the corpus. In short, comparing the percentages of the three steps for Move 2 "Establishing a niche", it can be concluded that most of the non-native writers prefer to add "to what is known" compared to "Indicating a gap" and "presenting positive justifications."

In correspond to the findings on Move 1 and 2, it is suggested that more emphasis and caution on utilizing Move 2 Step 1A "Indicating a gap" is to be given in the teaching of writing using CARS model [6] to computer science writers in Malaysia.

Move 3 is occurs in 91% of the articles. While the overall percentage for Move 3 is high, the percentages of the steps indicated that some of the steps are underutilized. Step 1 for Move 3 "Announcing present research descriptively and/or purposively" has been underutilized at only 86% compared to 98% in Shehzad [24]. Move 3 Step 2 has also been utilized in a smaller percentage compared to the study by Shehzad [24]. Only 1% of the corpus opts for this strategy compared to 32% in Shehzad [24]. Move 3 Step 3 "Definitional clarifications" and Move 3 Step 4 "Summarizing methods" are realized at 17 and 53%, respectively. However, percentages from the previous studies on computer science articles are not available for comparison because these steps are newly added in CARS 2004 model [6], whereas most of the studies used CARS 1990 model [5].

The steps in Move 3 are less fixed in orders and may appear before one or another. Swales [6] suggested that Steps 5–7 are possible in some field but may also be unlikely in others. In this study, Move 3 Step 5 "Announcing principle outcomes" is realized in only 15% of the corpus. The percentage of 15% is alarmingly low as the utilization of this step in studies on computer science research articles suggested that this step is realized at higher percentage of 73% in [24], 70% in [14], and 75% in Anthony [33]. Furthermore, Shehzad [24] suggested that this step is an obligatory strategy for computer science articles. Move 3 Step 6 "Stating the value of the present research" is also underutilized at 35% compared to 55% by Shehzad [24]. This step is recommended as an obligatory step in computer science research article; however, the non-native writers in this study prefer to skip this strategy. In addition to the low percentages in Steps 5 and 6, Move 3 Step 7 "Outlining the structure of the paper" is also realized at a low percentage of 34% compared to the other studies with 86% [24], 70% [14], and 83.3% [33]). Following the low utilization when compared to the other computer science corpus, Move 3 Steps 5–7 must be emphasized in the writing classroom for computer science non-native writers in Malaysia.

In this section, the findings on the use of citation in Move 1 are presented. First, the percentage on the citation used for move 1 was given, and then, the excerpts that showed the severity of not utilizing this step in Move 1 is explained. After that, the percentages of occurrence for Move 1 according to the university group and journal type are given.

Another phenomenon discovered in this study is the use of citation for Move 1. CARS model [6] posits that Move 1 is to be accompanied by citations. However, it was discovered that even though the research articles fulfilled the strategy on establishing the research territory by making topic generalization and increasing the specificity of the topic, many of the research articles did not have the required citation. Twenty-five research articles or 16.7% of the research articles have delayed the citation up to the fifth sentence and as late as the 17th sentence. The details on the citation in the Introduction section are summarized in the table below.

	Count	Percentage
Realization of Move 1	141	94
Move 1 with citation	96	64
Move 1 with delayed citation	25	16.7
Move 1 with no citation	22	14.7
No citation made in Introduction section	7	4.7

About 14.7% of Move 1 made in the research articles did not have any citation at all; instead, the citation only appeared in Move 2 where the discussion has developed to the research niche level. More surprisingly, 4.7% or seven of the research articles did not include any citation at all in the entire Introduction section. Only 64% of the research articles in the corpus used citation as suggested in CARS model [6].

"Data development meta-analysis (DEM) is a prevailing instrument for measuring the operation of system organizations and the functioning sections of components. DEM includes the parameters of many research areas particularly in system operation, management of data, organizational behavior, operational research, finance, and statistics. DEM is a multi-parametric procedure for calculating the qualified competences of a set of developed management protocols (DMPs), which uses a number of inputs to produce a number of outputs. The focus is to assess the comparative competence of the homogenous DMPs by expending the proportion of the outputs to the measured sum of inputs. It specifies the usual competence capacity from a single input to a number of inputs. *This method was initially introduced by Anas (1978) and popularized by Amber, Cain, and Bates (1988) (ACB model).*"

The need for citations even during the initial part of the introduction is necessary, even when the topic is being written on the general level. When the writers establish the research territory by writing on the general topics, the writers are addressing a bigger readership compared to writing directly on the research niche. By addressing on the general domain first, bigger readership can be expected [32] and then by writing with increasing specificity to the niche, this group of readership can be drawn to the niche of the study. If the writer dives straight to writing on the niche, some readers who are not familiar with the terms of the niche may be put off, not realizing the possible link and extension that the particular niche has with the readers' research interest [35]. As such by missing citations in Move 1, the research article may miss out a number of potential readers and future citations. Given that Move 1 provides the link and extension with the bigger research domain and readership, it is understood why CARS model (2004) explicitly posits that citation as an obligatory strategy. Citation must be used especially when citing the previous work at this point to establish the association and connection to what Shehzad ([24] p. 22) described as the "research cult." The following example is used to illustrate the importance of citation, even when at the initial level of establishing the research territory.

In this excerpt, the citation has been delayed to the sixth sentence which is in line 12. The Introduction begins with Move 1 by giving description on the general research topic which is DEM. And then, the research article offers a definition for DEM, and this definition is considered as Move 1, not Move 3 Step3 which is "definitional clarifications." The reason is because the niche of the research article based on the title is "decision-making units" and "fuzzy concept", so the term being defined is still at topic generalization level and not yet at the specific niche level. Notice that the citation only comes in after a few sentences later. No citation was made for the definition, description, or comments on the general topic. The citation is considered delayed because citations on the definition, description, and comments could have linked the writing to the existing literature and body of research. Having the citation delayed caused the connection and association to be established at a later reading sequence and appeared less connected to the existing body of research.

In short, delay or omission of citation in Move 1 is a deficiency and may appear like a lack of involvement and ambiguous ownership of ideas.

The findings on the use of citation suggest that the utilization of Move 1 for this group of non-native writers needs to be improved. Even though Move 1 has been utilized by the writers, there is room for improvement on the use of citation for this move because the citation has been delayed and omitted in some of the research articles.

5. Conclusion

In short, the patterns of the findings indicate the common moves and steps that are being utilized by the Malaysian writers. The underutilized steps have also been identified and thus suggested the need for more emphasis and caution in the application of CARS model in teaching writing for the particular group. While the findings indicated the applicability of CARS model [6], the description on how the moves and steps are utilized in target publication is still needed; particularly when many English teachers are not content experts in computer science discipline.

The model for research article provided a common guideline for authors to follow. While journal type plays an important factor in the selection of strategies, the highly cited research articles showed that the strategies recommended in the model is still prevalent. Given that the findings of the studies shows that non-native writer underutilized some of the important strategies, writing instructors and non-native writers must be cautioned and reminded on using these strategies. The underutilized strategies must be explained, particularly on what the strategies are and how the strategies can be realized. The assertiveness on accomplishing the strategies must be taught and reminded by the instructors.

Author details

Ina Suryani*, Mohd Mustafa Al Bakri Abdullah and Hazry Desa
Universiti Malaysia Perlis, Perlis, Malaysia

*Address all correspondence to: inasuryani@unimap.edu.my

References

[1] Aksnes DW, Rip A. Researchers' perceptions of citations. Research Policy. 2009;**38**(6):895-905

[2] Antonakis J, Bastardoz N, Liu Y, Schriesheim CA. What makes articles highly cited? The Leadership Quarterly. 2014;**2**(1):152-179

[3] Didegah F, Thelwall M. Determinants of research citation impact in nanoscience and nanotechnology. Journal of the American Society for Information Science and Technology. 2013;**64**(5):1055-1064

[4] Ina S, Aizan Y, Noor Hashima AA. Introduction sections of research articles with high and low citation indices. Pertanika Journal of Social Sciences and Humanities. 2015;**23**(4):1139-1152

[5] Swales JM, Najjar H. The writing of research article introductions. Written Communication. 1987;**4**(2):175-191

[6] Swales JM. Genre Analysis: English for Academic and Research Settings. Cambridge: Cambridge University Press; 1990

[7] Swales JM. Research Genres: Explorations and Applications. New York: Cambridge University Press; 2004

[8] Hirano E. Research article introductions in English for specific purposes: A comparison between Brazilian Portuguese and English. English for Specific Purposes. 2009;**28**(4):240-250

[9] Bhatia V. Applied genre analysis: A multi-perspective model. Revista de la Asociación Europea de Lenguas para Fines Específicos. 2002;**4**:3-19

[10] Ahmad UK. Scientific research articles in Malay: A situated discourse analysis [PhD]. US: University of Michigan; 1997

[11] Safnil A. Rhetorical structure analysis of the Indonesian research articles [PhD]. Canberra: The Australian National University; 2000

[12] Adnan Z. Some potential problems for research articles written by Indonesian academics when submitted to international English language journals. The Asian EFL Journal Quarterly. 2009;**11**(1):109-127

[13] Salom LG, Monreal CS, Olivares MC. The move-step structure of the introductory sections of Spanish PhD theses. Revista Española de Lingüística Aplicada. 2008;**21**:85-106

[14] Kanoksilapatham B. Rhetorical structure of biochemistry research articles. English for Specific Purposes. 2005;**24**(3):269-292

[15] Suryani I, Hanani A, Zubir F. The use of citation in establishing the research territory by writers of Malay language journals. In: Proceeding 11th International Technology, Education and Development Conference (INTED 2017); 6-8 March 2017; Valencia, Spain. 2017. DOI: 10.21125/inted.2017.2023

[16] Posteguillo S. The schematic structure of computer science research articles. English for Specific Purposes. 1999;**18**(2):139-160

[17] Shehzad W. Introduction of computer science research paper: Divergence from CARS. Kashmir Journal of Language Research. 2012;**15**(2):19-39

[18] Jogthong C. Research article introductions in Thai: Genre analysis of academic writing [Doctoral dissertation]. West Virginia University; 2001

[19] Mirahayuni NK. Investigating textual structure in native and non-native English research articles: Strategy differences between English and Indonesian writers [PhD]. Australia: University of New South Wales; 2002

[20] Shehzad W. Announcement of the principal findings and value addition in computer science research papers. Revista de la Asociación Europea de Lenguas para Fines Específicos. 2010;**19**:97-118

[21] Shehzad W. Corpus based genre analysis: Computer science research article introductions [PhD dissertation]. Islamabad, Pakistan: National University of Modern Languages; 2005

[22] Samraj B. Introductions in research articles: Variations across disciplines. English for Specific Purposes. 2002;**21**(1):1-17

[23] Sheldon E. Rhetorical differences in RA introductions written by English L1 and L2 and Castilian Spanish L1 writers. Journal of English for Academic Purposes. 2011;**10**(4):238-251. DOI: 10.1016/j.jeap.2011.08.004

[24] Shehzad W. How to end an introduction in a computer science article? A corpus-based approach. Language and Computers. 2006;**60**(1):227-241

[25] Ministry of Higher Education. Amanat Tahun 2010 Pengajian tinggi ke arah transformasi negara. Putrajaya, Malaysia: Kementerian Pengajian Tinggi; 2011

[26] Patton MQ. Qualitative Evaluation and Research Methods. Thousand Oaks: SAGE Publications, Inc.; 1990

[27] Shehzad W. Explicit author in the scientific discourse: A corpus-based study of the author's voice. Malaysian Journal of ELT Research. 2007;**3**:56-73

[28] Suryani I, Yaacob A, Aziz NHA, Ariffin Z. Comparing the rhetorical strategies in the research articles of two computer science journals. In: Proceeding for 11th International Technology, Education and Development Conference (INTED 2017); 6-8 March 2017; Valencia, Spain. 2017. DOI: 10.21125/inted.2017.2018

[29] Roosfa H, Yahya M. The impact of E-journals on the Malaysian scholarly community. In: Proceeding for Orcun 15th International Conference; Istanbul: Electronic Publishing. 2011. pp. 158-164

[30] Singh PK, Thuraisingam T, Nair V, David M. The research imperative in the evolving environment of public universities in Malaysia Parvin. The Journal of the South East Asia Research Centre. 2013;**5**(1):1-18

[31] MyCite MCC. Malaysian Journal of Computer Sciences; Malaysian Citation Center, Ministry of Education. 2014. Available from: http://www.myjurnal.my/publish/MJCS/index.php [Accessed: May 20, 2014]

[32] Suryani I, Zubir F, Ghazali N, Aclan E, Yaacob A. Differences in writing research article introductions among the Academics in Private Universities. In: Proceeding for EDULEARN18; Palma de Mallorca, Spain. 2018. pp. 10988-10993. DOI: 10.21125/edulearn.2018.2709

[33] Anthony L. Writing research article introductions in software engineering: How accurate is a standard model? IEEE Transactions on Professional Communication. 1999;**42**(1):38-46

[34] Ina S, Yacob A, Abd Aziz NH. "Indicating a Research Gap" in Computer Science Research Article Introductions by Non-Native English

Writers. Asian Social Science. 2015;**11**(28):293

[35] Suryani I, Rashid SA, Hussin K, Yaacob A, Hashima N. Rhetorical Comparison of the Promotional Strategies Used in Performing Arts and Visual Arts Research Articles. In: Proceedings of the 2nd International Colloquium of Art and Design Education Research (i-CADER 2015). Singapore: Springer; 2016. pp. 319-327

Chapter 6

Human Behavior Modeling: The Necessity of Narrative

Roger Parker

Abstract

As progress is made in the development of artificial intelligent mechanisms to assist human research into aspects of industrial, biomechanical and biomedical engineering, the conceptualization of mental behavior of human entities become more vital and more central to the success of any interaction between machine and humans. This discussion explores one of the most important features of human behavior, the fundamental and irreversible concept of narrative. The narrative is the essential construct for the theoretical understanding and presentation of human communication, including formal and informal logic, emotional wonder and desperation, noble and selfish biases, nationalism and globalist politics, and any form of spiritualism. This presentation offers a working definition of human narrative and proposes its basic structure that must be represented by any computer system which is required to deal with human behavior.

Keywords: human behavior modeling, narrative definition and structure, computer-human communications, logic modeling, bias modeling, emotional modeling, human agent-based modeling

1. Introduction

Artificial intelligence has made significant gains in operational context in the last two decades. One area of success has been demonstrated by the widespread implementation of agent-based modeling (ABM). Used extensively in a variety of contexts, there has been increased interest in the implementation of ABM's where the agents represent the behavior of individual or groups of human beings in a social context. This leads to the application of the irreversible concept of narrative [1]. The narrative is a fundamental concept for the theoretical understanding and presentation of virtually any kind of human behavior. Our discussion here presents an abstract, yet working, definition of the narrative. A basic structure that must be incorporated into any computer system which is required to deal with human behavior is offered, and the implications of that structure in a variety of human contexts are examined.

This approach to agent-based modeling has been in development for nearly two decades now. The first demonstration of the context in which a narrative became an essential part of a software system was created by AirMarkets Corporation, a collaboration of individuals from the air travel industry. It simulates the behavior of individuals and groups that have elected to fly from one city to another, including when they are going to fly, how much each is going to pay, and how likely any particular flight option is [2].

The work supporting the initial formulation, resulted from extensive research by the author and his associates, culminating in the writing and publication of a doctoral thesis under the tutorage of global experts at the University of Technology in Sydney, Australia [3]. At that time artificial intelligence was still in its infancy, and the development of pattern recognition and the emergence of artificial intelligence technology based on such capability has since argued for the consideration of human-replacement computer systems. But artificial intelligence technology has a great deal of work to do before it can even come close to replacing ordinary humans, or even a broad class of animal life, in any kind of depth. This presentation gives a substantial indication of how far we have to go.

The next section of the discussion describes the narrative construct. The notion of event, time, and associated probability are essential concepts. We then incorporate these important narrative ideas used routinely in mathematical and computer models and simulation. These concepts are exemplified by a range of rational choice models, common to artificial intelligence computer development, but viewed from the perspective of human behavior modeling. This approach is illustrated briefly in the next section, which describes in overview form the AirMarkets Simulation, which is a computer program that represents the booking of over 40 million travelers on the world's commercial airline system using an agent-based, narrative structured methodology. We then move to a survey of heuristic choice model concepts, followed by an exploration of even more human—and less computer—narrative structures, including social network protocols and sources of bias in human narrative execution.

We close with a review of future needed work, including mention of several mathematical theorems that limit the applicability of relevant software development regarding computer-based narrative software and distinctions between human and computer-based analysis that such analyses imply.

2. A formal notion of narrative

The objective of this research is to develop computing machine ability to represent behavior in an agent-based software architectural context, so we can build agent-based models of activity such as market behavior, political contexts, or social interaction. Our first consideration is the creation of a framework for describing how human behavior can be characterized in a fashion consistent with observed patterns while dynamic enough to describe actions and activities that exist only, at least at some point in time, in the imagination of the individual. And time is an essential feature of such a characterization, since all behavior (of virtually all mobile biological entities) is selected, observed, enacted, realized, or even is cited as existing occurs over some distinct and evident time period. In addition, we want the description of the framework to be able to differentiate between what happens within the creature, such as choices based on memory or mental understanding, and external to the agent, such as weather and the behavior of other agents. That is, the construct must describe the relationship between what an agent *perceives* the world to be and what the world *actually* is.

Virtually all animal organisms show evidence of memory-based pattern creation and maintenance. In his fun discussion Montague [4] makes the case that virtually all biological entities that can move about has some ability to forecast at least the immediate future, and therefore must have at least a basic mental image of what the effect of its future activity is likely to be. The creature compares the perceived state of its current environment with its internal understanding of it and uses a cause-and-effect chain to determine what it expects the future state of the environment will be if it undertakes some appropriate activity. The phrase *cause-and-effect* refers to an internal conception by the creature that the state of affairs perceived by the creature as currently the case is due, in large part, to relationships between things that occurred in the past and the current state, and the anticipated future state of affairs that will exist if the creature does some appropriate thing. It is this internal, mental construct that we call a *narrative*. Indeed, for the artificial intelligence purposes of this discussion, the definition of narrative that applies to the modeling of human agents is as follows: *The term 'narrative' will be taken to mean a pattern maintained internally by an agent that represents temporal cause-and-effect chains which define events that are perceived by the agent, with which the agent 'understands' the events, and based on which the agent takes action*. Since narratives are temporal cause and effect chains maintained in a mental structure, they are essentially independent of the reality they represent.

Narratives are favorite topics of people who are interested in human creative activity, so much of the insight into their nature come from authors, poets, playwrights and composers. The term *narratology* is used to identify such discussions. Danto [5] defines the term *atomic* narrative to be a single event with related past and future. **Figure 1** is an illustration of the concept. Note that there is past and future narrative time, and the event has a history and a range of outcomes.

This is the state space that obtained before the event occurs. To the right is an arc representing the set of possible outcomes of the event. An atomic narrative can have a set of *discrete* outcomes, a *continuous* range of outcomes, as shown in **Figure 2**, or, at least theoretically, a mixture of the two. The history here, of course, is history in narrative time, and compared with history in real time, is woefully incomplete. That is, there must exist states in real time history that are not in a narrative history, no matter how thorough the recording of that history might be. The actual content of the existence of reality is never completely known to humans because we are unable to completely absorb and understand a description of reality in a finite interval of time.

That there can be more than one possible outcome is a vital property of the event. An event occurs when something in reality changes because the agent recognizing and responding to the event promulgates the change. The change is actually realized as an event outcome. There is a family of probability distributions associated with the outcome set of every event. This family is a stochastic process indexed by a set of narrative variables referred to as *resources* and is thus called the *event stochastic process*. The stochastic process can be denoted $P_\Lambda(Y/X)$ which is the probability that outcome Y occurs given history X and resource allocation Λ. A *molecular* narrative is simply of a sequence (in time) of atomic narratives and a narrative can be made up of multiple molecular narratives that are simultaneous in narrative time. A narrative that contains such multiple molecular narratives is called

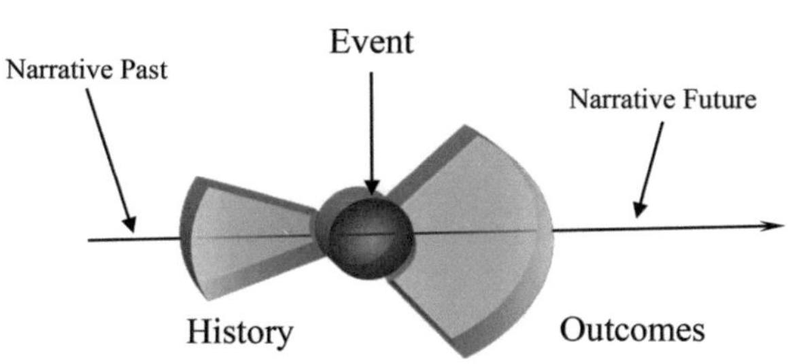

Figure 1.
Schematic conceptualization of an atomic narrative.

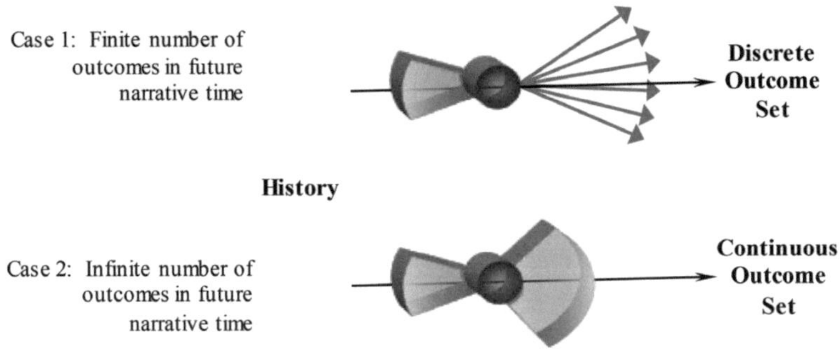

Figure 2.
Discrete and continuous outcome sets.

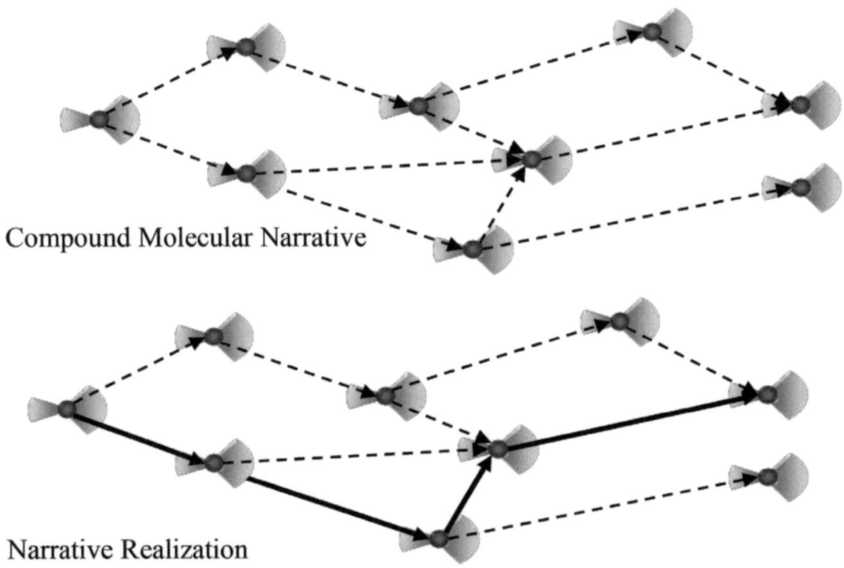

Figure 3.
Molecular narratives.

compound and is illustrated in **Figure 3**. As real time transpires, the course of the narrative is *realized*, which is illustrated in **Figure 3** with the solid line connecting the relevant events.

Thus, narratives are memory structures that are retrieved under a currently perceived state configuration. The retrieval is not only representative of the present, but also reflects the relevant past and future. The future portion of the narrative is created from the expectation property created by the probability associated with the narrative. If one outcome results, the narrative will go one course, while if a different one results, it will follow a different path. The narrative carries with it a description of the expected consequences of these event outcomes. Thus, the description of the future consists of a set of branches, each opening a new course for the narrative to take. Furthermore, there is a probability distribution associated with each potential outcome which dictates a probability that the branch initiated by that outcome will be realized.

It should be noted that the stochastic structure of the probabilities cannot be assumed to be simple. The likelihood of outcome *A* vs. outcome *B* may depend on outcomes that were the result of previous events or sets of previous events. More succinctly, every atomic narrative has a probability distribution associated with its outcomes, but the distribution associated with the outcome of the last atomic narrative in a molecular narrative is not independent of the other atomic narratives which make up the molecular narrative. Therefore, every narrative has a past which contains the information required to support the future outcome stochastic processes.

But the narrative past is not a completely accurate description of what lead to the present and is conditioning the future. It has inaccuracies caused by imperfect recall and incomplete data. Memory deteriorates as events recede into the past, and hence there must be a probability associated with the accuracy of the recall, and hence the past of a narrative also has an associated stochastic process structure. This is illustrated in **Figure 4**. The past and the future are shown as the widening ends of a hyperbolic cone representing the increasing uncertainty surrounding the past and future of the narrative, and the present is the narrowest part of the hyperbolic surface. The small circles connected by the lines inside the hyperbolic solid represent the events of the narrative and their relationships, as perceived at that point in the narrative. These event conditions change from past to future, but the degree of uncertainty in the narrative increases as the past recedes and the looming distant future is contemplated. This results in the loss of resolution of the event description.

The individual that creates and maintains a narrative is called its *owner*. All narratives have owners, and all narratives are unique, to a greater or lesser extent, to their owners. But narratives are also shared. Language and communications are important adaptive tools for the human species and a vital purpose served by language is the sharing of narratives. Indeed, some suggest [6] it is the sole purpose of language, since all communications in his view is the description of a narrative. Shared narratives are not, however, perfect copies held by each individual that is, part of the sharing group. Each individual owner at least modifies the shared narrative structure to fit their own unique set of compound narratives that include the shared one. Moreover, shared narratives become institutionalized into laws, codes of conduct, norms, and other social constructions that serve to assist in group adaptation and evolution. Shared narratives are a very powerful social and evolutionary tool. In fact, it could be argued that the interconnections of the atomic narratives that make up shared compound narratives may set the framework for the multilevel selection adaptation evidenced by group evolution. While beyond the

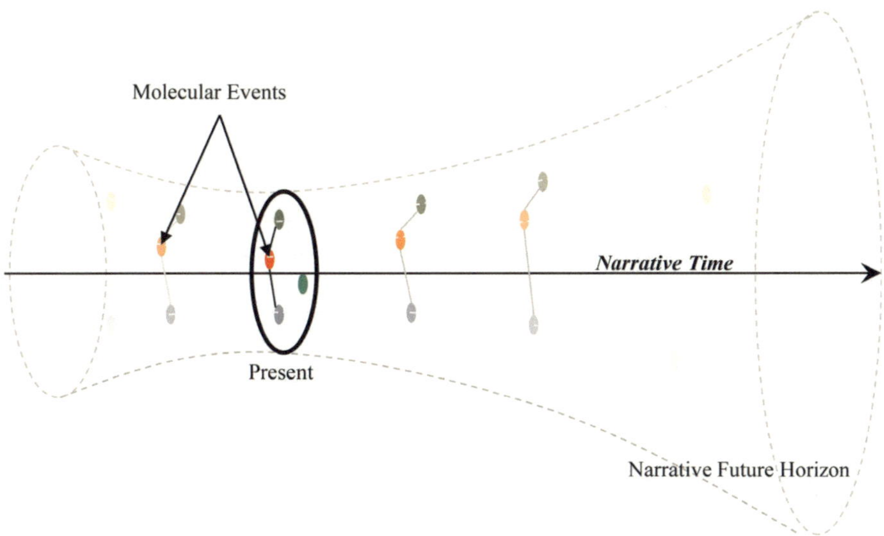

Figure 4.
The time structure of narratives.

scope of this discussion, future research in this area using computer-based agents designed with the narrative construct might yield very useful results. It also should be noted that other modes of communications aside from formal speech are also available both to humans and to other species. Indeed, the question arises as to whether or not there is some form of communications available to plants?

It is reasonable to conclude that narratives are mechanisms that result from human evolution. Much like the arguments presented by Sober and Wilson [7] and Shermer [8], the narrative hypothesis can be reinforced by evolutionary feasibility and their proven success as an adaptive device in support of both individual and group survival. This leads to the inference that the outcome of a narrative is either *desirable* or *undesirable*. Some are very simple, like what to have for lunch. At the other extreme, compound narratives that support religious beliefs and institutions can be invoked to portray a future where death is merely a change in physical state from this world to another, which may be Heaven (desirable), Purgatory (not so well favored) or Hell (clearly undesirable). Given this property of desirability, narratives then can be considered to be the vehicle by which value is expressed by the individual, and it is from narratives that values arise as identifiable attributes of human behavior.

The narrative framework can be considered as a storage device for not only memories, but also expectations. The role of expectation in narrative structure—the projection of the effect associated with some cause in the future—is quite clear. The maintenance of a set of expectations associated with the various outcomes in a particular event-based choice situation is required for the mental storage of such expectations. It is implying too much inherent human analytic ability to assert that each such expectation set has a formal probability distribution also maintained as part of its mental representation, especially since such distributions would be dependent on the pathway by which the event itself arose, and not only on the fact that the event came about at all. Nonetheless, narratives provide both a context and framework within which expectation can be stored, recalled and manipulated. However, for the purposes of modeling human agents, the expectation-storage property is important. Indeed, one of the most useful applications of an agent model might be that both the "correct (logical)" application of probabilities, or the "deficient (logically false but commonly held)," expectation distributions can be modeled, and the results as expressed in specific choice contexts compared.

A human individual is part of a world and is in constant interaction with it. The intervention in the real world by the agent occurs by means of the allocation resources to the event at hand in order to alter its perceived probability distribution of the outcomes, either toward those it favors, or away from those it dislikes. In this way, the values held in the narrative are expressed in action. Since compound narratives are molecular, and thus made up of sequences of atomic narratives, any attempt by an agent to affect what it thinks will be the desired course of a narrative involves choosing a specific outcome from the set of outcomes of the narrative representation of that event. And it must do so one event at a time. Otherwise contradictions, uncontrolled feedback, process deadlock or other dangerous anomalies would emerge. *Thus, in the narrative framework, the relationship between the narrative owner and its environment is always an event, and therefore always a choice problem*. And there are a number of other issues of interest, but beyond the scope of this discussion. What about the time it takes to select outcomes? What happens during that selection process? And what about the cost of being wrong? Or how does the narrative accommodate the shifting environment.

Notice there is absolutely no requirement that any of the events or sequences of events described by a narrative be true, in the sense that there is Karl Popper's intersubjective verifiability of narrative content [9]. Indeed, everyone has experienced erratic and unpredictable behavior on the part of others. Such behavior is seen because the narrative driving the erratic individual is different in some important way from what the observer expects, given her constellation of narratives. Since narratives exist as neurological entities (fundamentally memories), study of their physical existence and attendant properties resides in the domain of the neuroscientist. But what is represented by the narrative pattern, and whether or not that has any reality outside of the narrative itself, is an entirely separate question. It can be as fanciful or factual as the owner wishes and is capable of managing. The fact that fanciful narratives can be as real as factual ones creates the conditions on which wonderful fiction can be portrayed, both in books, on television, and in the theatre. It also creates the capability for popular politicians and dangerous authoritarians to put forth absurd and violent behaviors as within human and normal perspectives. Simply review the history of political activity in Europe prior to World War II.

With respect to building a computer program, there is a minimal organization required for the implementation of a narrative in the context of agent-based modeling. The general definition of agent has been presented in Parker and Bakken [10] and in Parker and Perroud [11]. For our purposes, agents will always be implemented in the form of computer programs. Within the agent are mechanisms for perceiving the environment, making choices about what to do given the environmental information and from the context of the agent's motivating narrative, and taking actions that advance the agent's narrative. This simple agent structure consists of four components and is illustrated in **Figure 5**.

Corresponding to the memory for a human being, the *state vector* is an array of variables which describe the current state of the agent. Referring to this array as a vector does not imply that it is necessarily a precise set of real numbers laid out in a row or column manner. Structures more complex than simple numbers can be specified. However, it does imply the memory object is both precisely well-defined and finite. The state vector also encodes the appropriate narrative structures that represent the beliefs and aspirations of the agent being considered. For example, it contains the probability distributions of the outcome sets relevant to the events the agent will encounter during the simulation. The state vector is maintained as appropriately defined data structure.

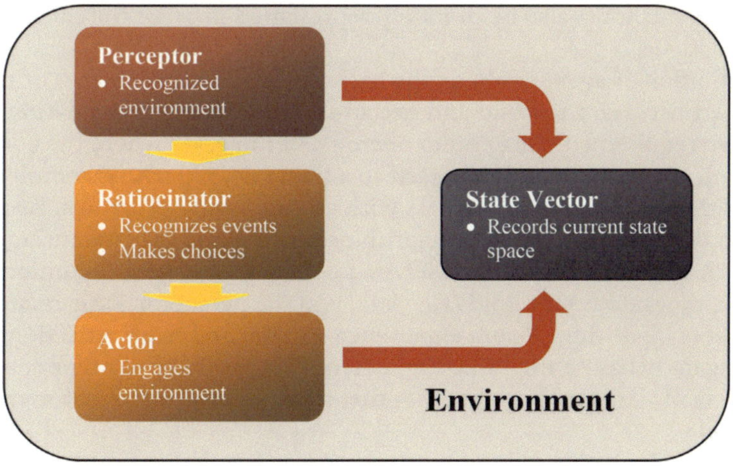

Figure 5.
The general structure of an agent.

Like the ability of humans to receive, filter and understand information, a computer agent can receive information about the current conditions in its environment through the code component called the *perceptor*. Almost without exception, perceptors are message-handling routines the purpose of which is to 'observe' the current state of the agent's environment, and filter and translate that information into a form that can be used by the choice-making component of the agent, converting the messages from the environment into an internal form of use to the agent. This internal translation is unique to each agent, which thus allows for agents that interpret the same external message differently. This would be important if different agents have different narrative events that were triggered by the same external environmental conditions.

The actions of the agents to external messages, both those which are put into the environment as output messages by other agents, those required for changes in the internal state vector of the agent, and those that require the attention of other agents, are managed by the *ratiocinator* component. The ratiocinator makes choices and adapts the behavior of the agent. This is the part of the agent which replicates how the human intersects with the simulated world in accordance with the then-active narrative structure. How such stochastic choice mechanisms are implemented are within the purview of the agent's ratiocinator.

When it is required that an agent create input to other components of the agent-based simulation, it can issue messages out to the environment by way of what we call an *actor*. It specifically engages the agent environment. Messages intended for other agents are detected by those agents as they interact with the environment.

For even the simplest case of the atomic narrative with a single event, the agent components must contain significant data. The perceptor needs to be designed to recognize the occurrence of the event and the perceived state of the environment at the time of the occurrence. The ratiocinator must be programmed to perform one of a set of choice protocols the agent will apply to exercise the choice required by the event, including the availability and allocation conditions of the resources at the agent's disposal. And the actor must have, in its repertoire of possible actions, those that are suitable given the event perception and protocol requirements. If the narrative construct driving the event recognition and intervention is a molecular narrative, with a number of events connected in a time-ordered and contingency network, then each atomic narrative must be delineated as described above. Furthermore, the connections between the component events must also be precisely represented in order to reliably represent the agent's actions.

This definition of agent contains the basic outline of all the pieces of the programmer's art necessary to build and execute a virtual market simulation. At first glance, these requirements may seem onerous. But in cases where the construct has been applied, the problem reduces itself to a tractable, if perhaps complex, computer algorithm programming task. As with all computing programs, two elements are present: the data on which the algorithms operate and the computing code which executes the algorithms themselves. Looking at the agent definition from that perspective, the state vector holds the data, and the perceptor, ratiocinator and actor consist of algorithms. From experience to date, and from reflection of how a particular agent behavior might be implemented in a variety of other contexts, the programming of the choice protocol set that resides in the ratiocinator seems the most daunting.

Why do care in the least about narratives? Because they represent—in fact are the existential structure—of what us advanced species of humans refer to as models. Now let us look at that!

3. Modeling and simulation

Human beings think in terms of mental models of the world around them and their relationship to it [12]. We formulate concepts and ideas and link them together to represent the way we think the world works in some significant regard and use those representations to make decisions on our future actions. These models can range from simple statements of assumed cause and effect—"if I step out in front of a moving bus, there's a good chance I could be seriously hurt"—through physical scale models of buildings or vehicles in their design stages through mathematical representations of complex social or physical systems. Common to models of whatever composition or subject is that they are *abstractions*, and therefore *simplifications*, of reality, retaining what is believed to be salient features of the problem at hand.

We are only concerned with models that are represented mathematically, either in the form of one or more equations or as a computer program. Consider the simple "What if?" scenario analysis applied to the results from a conjoint analysis, or more elaborate "war games" in which competing teams of managers (or MBA students) develop and implement strategies in an interactive fashion. An underlying principle of modeling is the representation of one process or set of processes with a simpler process or set of processes. The Monopoly® board game, for example, reduces a complex economic system into a limited set of transactions. Part of the fun of playing the game derives from the degree to which the outcomes (wealth accumulation and bankruptcy) resemble the outcomes from a real-world process that is, sort of being simulated.

An important concept regarding simulation is time. This temporal property is an essential characteristic of process-representative simulation and differentiates the application of simulation as an analytic and scientific tool from many other approaches, such as deductive logic or statistical inference. As noted in the previous section, the central role of time is also an integral part of agent-based model simulations. With an express representation of time, the dynamics of a system can be explicitly studied.

In many circumstances, the phenomenon under investigation cannot be ethically or safely subjected to experimentation. The study of disease epidemics, social intolerance and military tactics are obvious examples. In many situations the scale of the process under study prohibits any other approach. In astronomy and astrophysics, the universe is not available for experimental manipulation, but a simulation of important aspects of it are available for such study. Similarly, explorations of cultural development or species evolution cannot be executed with physical laboratory environment, while a simulation permits hypothesis testing and inference on a reasonable time scale. Finally, some systems are so complex that traditional experimental science seems hopeless as a research approach. Among these systems are ecological dynamics and evolutionary economics.

Figure 6 lays out the "ethnology" of mathematical modeling in general and simulation modeling in particular, starting with the invention of the calculus in the 1700s and continuing up to the present day. (This diagram is adapted from Gilbert and Troitszch [13].) The two broad categories of stochastic and deterministic simulation models are indicated by the shaded ovals. The bold face labels define the mathematical contexts of the various modeling formalizations, while their genealogy is spelled out with the lines. As illustrated in this diagram, agent-based simulation belongs to the class of stochastic simulations and descended from a form of simulation called *discrete-event* simulations. Discrete event simulations are stochastic simulations that attempt to mimic the behavior of the discrete parts of a system and

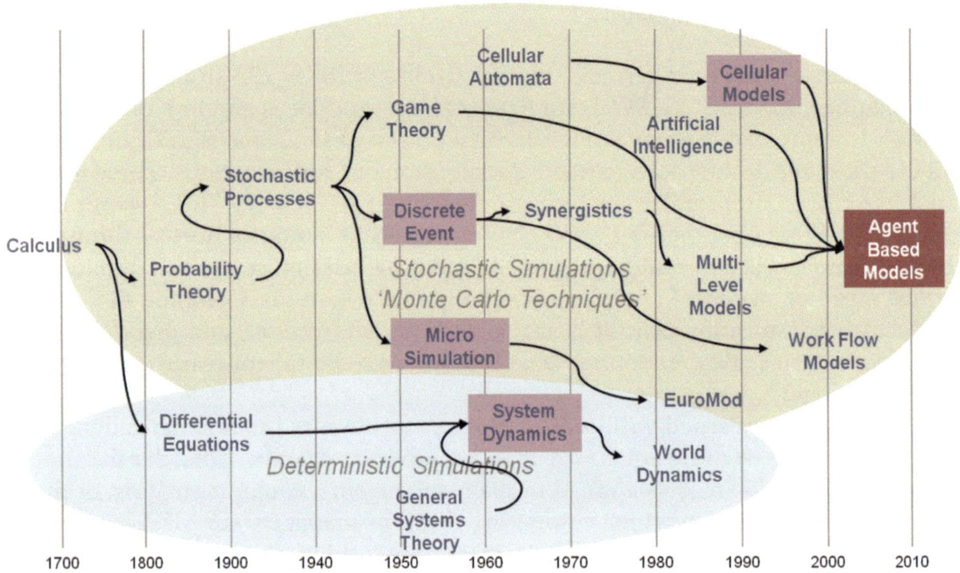

Figure 6.
The ethnology of mathematical modeling and simulation.

their interaction. As indicated in **Figure 6**, a number of other varieties of simulation have evolved from the discrete event form.

Also contributing to the heritage of agent simulation are game theory, artificial intelligence and cellular automata models. Some of the early applications of agent-based models were in the area of rational game play. Axelrod's [14] experiments with the prisoner's dilemma game is the classic example and is cited by virtually every practitioner of agent-modeling somewhere in their writings. Artificial intelligence models are a key component of the development of robotic systems (Wooldridge [15] is a chief proponent). If the behavior modeled by the discrete event simulation contains stochastic elements, as it usually does, then the simulation can be run repeatedly using random numbers generated by the relevant probability distributions, and the distributional characteristics of the resulting dynamics portrayed. In fact, for a system of even moderate scope this is the only way such dynamics can be validly studied. The ability to express dynamics through ordinary or stochastic partial differential equations can quickly exceed any reasonable closed form.

Mathematical models can be classified into two forms: *reductive* models and *structural* models. In a reductive model, a set of data is reduced to one or more equations or similar relationships that represent the data, but in a simpler, more parsimonious form. There is some loss of accuracy, the price of which is greater understandability. Linear regression is a ready example, where a set of pairs (or n-tuples) of data is replaced with an equation representing the relationship between the data values of one element of the set, called the dependent variable, as a linear combination of some collection of the other $(n-1)$-tuples, called independent variables. Structural models, on the other hand, are intended to be representations that not only reproduce patterns of observed data, but also characterize the process, or structure, by which the variables represented by the data relate to one another. Reductive models are not required to completely replicate the process by which the observed data is generated. They need only reproduce the observed results in a more economical and parsimonious way. Structural models focus on the way in which the observed values come about.

A good deal of applied mathematics and a substantial part of modern statistics is aimed at easing the problem of the generation of reductive models. Beyond linear regression, there are literally thousands of other applied techniques; Fourier series [16], time series analysis [17], discrete choice modeling (e.g., [18, 19]), and proportional hazard models [20] to name only a very few. Indeed, the so-called Stone-Weierstrass theorem in classical abstract analysis [21] describes a set of general conditions under which an arbitrary data set can be approximated to any desired degree of accuracy by a broad class of simpler functional forms. And reductive models are powerful and extremely useful tools. In econometrics, for example, reductive models are widely used for forecasting [22, 23]. For a thorough treatment of the structures and formal aspects of mathematical models, see Chang and Keisler [24].

But in the "harder" sciences like physics, reductive models give way to structural models. Newton's laws of motion, or Einstein's theories of relativity, are mathematical constructs which purport to not only represent the results of data sets arising from observations of natural phenomena, but also how the objects in the natural world interact with each other to generate the observed data. That is, the models do not merely represent the observations, but also describe the *process* by which the observations come about. As such, they carry more explanatory weight than reductive descriptions. They are more likely to be valid beyond the range of the initial observed data sets that lead to their formulation. Also, they have repeatedly been shown to be robust across varied data sets and when connected to other models which represent related systems.

Simulation is one of the more powerful structural modeling techniques. A simulation is a model which, by design, represents the relationships between entities in a system. In particular, a simulation captures the dynamics of the relationships between components of a system, reflecting how changes in one component create changes and affect the response of other components. Humphreys [25], in fact, defines a simulation as a structural model that explicitly includes time as a dimension, so that the dynamics between the variables described in the model can be appropriately portrayed.[1] The increasingly wide spread use of simulation also is tied to the development of computing power.

Note that the use of the word simulation here as a modeling technique should not be confused with the phrase when applied to certain methods of finding solutions to equations. For example, computing the volume of a complex solid in a multi-dimensional space, such as the area under a multi-dimensional normal probability distribution, can be done by generating a very large number of points in the relevant space and determining the ratio of those in the solid vs. those not in the solid.

Modeling and simulation which incorporates a definition of time (unidirectionality, non-repeatability, uncontrollability) are representations of narratives. Fisher incorporates the rationality of traditional logic into the narrative paradigm (with a somewhat critical slant):

> "Narrative rationality is not simply an account of the 'laws of thought,' nor is it normative in the sense that one *must* reason according to prescribed rules of calculation or inference making. Traditional rationality prescribes the way people should think when they reason truly or toward certainty. ... Traditional

[1] He uses time as the dimension carrying the dynamics, primarily because of its unidirectionality. Other dimensions, such as spatial coordinates, could also be used, but they do not necessarily have this unidirectional property.

rationality is, therefore, a normative construct. Narrative rationality is, on the other hand, descriptive; it offers an account, an understanding, of any instance of human choice and action, including science." [6].

How does this narrative construct relate in the modeling of human agents? As was stated earlier, the narrative provides the mechanism for separating reality from what the agent *thinks* is reality. That is, it defines the context, values and resources required to change the realization of a narrative to a desired outcome. Many consider individual narrative discovery as the central problem of marketing research, as exemplified by the strong methodological presence of ethnology in some marketing research quarters, such as ESOMAR (a European society of marketing research). It is clear that the choice process is a vital aspect of any such description. In fact, the narrative framework provides an ontological justification for pursuing the study of choice as the critical component of replicating the behavior of humans in agent-based models. It is not necessary to know the full constellation of narratives maintained by an individual to incorporate the concept into agent models. It is often sufficient, at least as a starting point, to model a few essential atomic narratives.

Narratives are needed for the construction of agents in a computing context because the distinction between the *reality* of the environment that an agent finds itself in and the *perception* and *interpretation* of that environment by the agent must be kept clear. Formally speaking, all narratives are models.[2] And, since a narrative is a sequence of events, there exists a finite sequence $\{1, 2, 3, \ldots, k\}$ such that each member of which has an associated stochastic process $E_i = P_{\Lambda(i)}(Y/X_i)$. So a narrative can be expressed as the ordered k-tuple $(E_1, E_2, E_3, \ldots, E_k)$, representing the possible outcomes of the narrative execution.

Narratives are to a significant degree a product of evolutionary history. As we observe human society across multiple cultures we should repeatedly encounter common behavioral attributes, since the environment in which humans have evolved have many essential elements in common. Moreover, we can then assert a behavioral universality that would support hypotheses that could be tested across cultures. Finally, if such universality can be supported, then the construction of agents that replicate important behavioral characteristics can be expected to be applicable in a wide range of contexts.

A thorough cataloging of human behavior patterns in cultures around the world has been assembled by the anthropology community. The University of Illinois at Urbana-Champaign maintains the Human Relations Area Files (HRAF), an organized and indexed compilation of every reported ethnographic study of human culture (UIUC [26]). Many scholars have used this resource in recent years to undertake cross-cultural studies of human behavior. Brown [27] has compiled a list of patterns of behavior that have been recorded in every human society that has been studied—anywhere in the world, large or small, old or modern. Brown focused on the hypothesis that a number of features of human culture would be found in all human experience, regardless of time, place, or history. When originally published, his views were sharply opposed to the prevailing anthropological wisdom. At the heart of the controversy was the nature-nurture debate, which still circulates actively today. Brown spent considerable space refuting the concept of cultural relativism, which holds that human cultures are vastly different with limitless variety.[3] Further, culture completely determines human behavior, and therefore

---

[2] But not all models are narratives. There is no need for a time dimension in every case.

[3] Cultural relativism *per se* became prominent in post-World War II sociological research largely in an attempt to refute the naïve "survival of the fittest" philosophy exemplified by the German Nazi era.

there can be no human universals. (For example, by taking a contrary view, Brown contradicted the great anthropologist Margaret Mead.[4]) This position is important for this analysis because, if there were no human traits that were independent of culture, then the problem of simulating human behavior with agents becomes extensively more difficult. In that case every culture would have a unique heritage and historical path, making generalization very difficult. Brown's refutation of the relativistic view of human behavior is therefore valuable to the arguments justifying agent modeling in computer science. If we cannot characterize human behavior in some reasonably perspicacious and parsimonious way, the task of defining human simulation agents will be significantly more onerous.

4. Rational choice protocols

Narratives are also the mechanisms by which agents communicate with each other—so-called shared narratives—and understand the world around them. They need not, however, be true descriptions of the world. All narratives are compounded from sequences of atomic events (are molecular narratives) and thus the choice process of the atomic narrative is the key focus. The set of choice protocols can be classified into four broad groups: (1) rational methods, including various concepts of bounded rationality, (2) heuristics, which are quick and easy (but often very inaccurate) rules-of-thumb, (3) social network protocols, which rely on communications between individuals to make choices, and (4) biases, which are significant errors often found in choice-making.

Consider what are usually referred to as protocols for *rational* choice. Perhaps the easiest of these would be rule-invocation methods. This is the situation where the agent making the choice has an available set of rules, and, depending on value of the state space when the event is encountered, one or more of these rules are used to determine the choice. Rule-based agents are widely used in agent-based models. Axelrod [14], Epstein [28], and Wooldridge [15] insist that rule-based agency is the wisest course of agent construction. This press for simplicity is in response to the need to explore and understand some of the unusual emergent results that are observed with agent-based models. A complicated agent structure makes analysis of such emergent structure much more arduous. And such a protocol is trivial to build into an agent. Merely specify the action to be engaged for each appropriate set of state space variable values. But this is not a *choice* protocol, since the outcome of the choice is predetermined by the rule set. It's a pre-defined action invocation, and since there is no probability associated with the rule-invocation, there can be no associated narrative event. Therefore, this kind of choice mechanism is not within the purview of agent-based models as defined here, which require such a stochastic mechanism.

The classic statistical decision problem is perhaps the oldest, and most 'rational' of this class of choice protocols. The fundamental problem of statistical decision theory is to select a possible action from a set of actions that minimizes expected loss. The loss function $L(a, \theta)$ associates a real-valued number (the loss) with an action a in some set of possible actions A and a state-space value $\theta \in \Theta$ (referred to as the *state of nature* in the statistical literature). The triple (Θ, A, L) represents the statistical decision problem. Generally, the choice at hand is which value of θ represents the "true" state of nature. Nominally, there exists empirical data

---

[4] Specifically, by pointing out that adolescents in Samoa indeed led stressful lives, just like teenagers everywhere else in the world.

represented by the random variable X (which could be a multidimensional entity), the probability distribution of which, $P_\theta(x)$ depends on this true state of nature. A decision rule d for a given value of the random variable X, say x, maps the value of one of the actions in A to x; that is, $d(x) \in A$. The loss is therefore the random quantity $L(\theta, d(x))$, and the expected value of $L(\theta, d(x))$, when θ is the actual state of nature, is called the risk function

$$R(\theta, d) = \mathrm{E}[L(\theta, d(X))] = \int_{x \in X} L(\theta, d(X)) dP_\theta(x). \tag{1}$$

The choice problem is to select the decision rule d from the set of all possible decision rules D that minimizes R. If it is assumed that each $d \in D$ is such that, for each $\theta \in \Theta$, the distribution function $F_X(x|\theta)$ is continuous on a set of probability one, then the above is the Lebesgue integral

$$R(\theta, d) = \int_{x \in X} L(\theta, d(X)) dF_X(x|\theta). \tag{2}$$

Ferguson [29] delineates a conceptualization of much of the field of statistics based on this definition, coupling it in with a game-theoretic construction. In fact, the triple (Θ, A, L) is a formal game in this sense.[5] It is easy to see that this is a quite well-defined problem. However, implementing that definition in a specific context can be a considerable endeavor. On the other hand, creating a computer routine to implement a statistical decision rule in an agent does not seem to be conceptually prohibitive, although it might require significant time and resources to build and execute.

In a general sense, all "rational" choice protocols are described by the statistical decision process defined above. Indeed, some would consider this formulation the axiomatic definition of a rational decision. This general formulation says nothing about the nature of the decision rules $d \in D$. They could be hugely complex or trivially simple. Moreover, the set of actions A can be finite or infinite. Much more familiar to the economic community is the choice process described in the random utility discrete choice case. The general formulation of this family of protocols is as follows. There exists a finite set J of possible choices with $\#(J)$ being the number of elements in the set J. Assume that the choices and the choosers are characterized by a vector of variables $\mathbf{z}_{ij}$ for decision-maker i and choice j. Each decision-making agent has an associated real-valued function $U_i(\mathbf{z}_{ij}) : J \to \mathcal{R}$ that assigns a *utility* to each choice. The alternative with the highest value of U_i is defined as the choice made, that is, the value j^* for which

$$U_i(\mathbf{z}_{ij*}) = \max_{j \in J} U_i(\mathbf{z}_{ij}) \tag{3}$$

This utility function is assumed to have an observable part $V_i(\mathbf{z}_{ij})$ and a stochastic component $\varepsilon_i(\mathbf{z}_{ij})$, and is therefore written as:

[5] Ferguson goes on to justify the application of Bayes' theory to statistics with his treatise, arguing that this game-theoretic perspective created a persuasive demonstration of the superiority of Bayesian statistical analysis. The text was written amid the roiling Bayes versus frequentist debate within the statistics community prominent in the latter half of the twntieth century, and which chugs along today with a steady, if tedious, background din.

$$U_i(\mathbf{z}_{ij}) = V_i(\mathbf{z}_{ij}) + \varepsilon_i(\mathbf{z}_{ij}). \tag{4}$$

Very often the $\varepsilon_i(\mathbf{z}_{ij})$ terms are assumed to have an Extreme Value Type 1 distributed with common location parameter γ (which, without loss of generality, can be set to zero) and common scale parameter μ. Then it can be shown ([17] p. 106) that

$$P_i(j^*) = \frac{e^{\mu V_i(\mathbf{z}_{ij*})}}{\sum_{j\in J} e^{\mu V_i(\mathbf{z}_{ij})}}, \tag{5}$$

The general discrete choice problem is based on the assumption that there exists a set of alternatives J with finite number of elements $\#(J)$. Furthermore, the agent making the choice has determined a complete preference order $\prec$ over the elements of J. A complete ordering on a set is a relation having the following conditions: [the idea is easier to understand by writing $a \prec b$ for $(a, b) \in \prec$, read as "a is less than or equal to b."]: (1) antisymmetry: if $a, b \in J$ and $a \prec b$, and $b \prec a$, then $a = b$; (2) reflexivity: for every $a \in A$ it is true that $a \prec a$; (3) transitivity: If $a \prec b$ and $b \prec c$ then $a \prec c$, and (4) completeness: for *every* pair $a, b \in A$ it is true that either $a \prec b$ or $b \prec a$. If the preference order fails to meet these conditions, then the utility function does not necessarily exist, and the discrete choice problem cannot be formulated in a utility maximization context.

However, human beings are not bound by the definitions of preference orders. Non-transitive, circular orderings are common. For example, when Mary is asked to choose between chocolate and vanilla ice cream, she selects chocolate. When asked her preference between vanilla and strawberry, she chooses vanilla, and when asked her choice between strawberry and chocolate, she prefers strawberry. The ordering is not transitive. This situation occurs because humans generally determine orderings pair-wise over some (possibly quite short) period of time, and the circular inconsistency is quite easy to manage if the time of the preference comparison can vary. Moreover, there's no reason why the completeness property needs to be met in real-life situations. (An ordering that does not meet the transitivity and complete conditions is termed a *partial ordering*.) Fortunately, it is possible to derive a set of completely ordered sets from any partially ordered set (by considering each completely ordered set as a separate entity, and ignoring singleton sets), so the utility maximization problem reduced to a bookkeeping issue, (assuming there is sufficient data to estimate the number of models that might arise). In some cases, the collection of completely ordered sets can be represented in a hierarchy. But the point is that agent designers do not need to insist on complete choice sets. In fact, any kind of pairing relationship can be used as a preference ordering, and each can have a unique (empirically derived) utility function.

The domain of rational choice models is not exhausted by the utility maximization of a discrete choice structure. Indeed, most choice situations are not even discrete, often requiring the selection of a parameter vector from a multiple-dimensioned real-valued vector space. Other methods are called upon here. Bayesian statistics have faded in and out of fashion over the past two centuries. Of special note are simulation approaches to statistical parameter estimation, confidence interval determinations, and hypothesis testing. In this context, the meaning of the word simulation is somewhat different from when it is applied to an agent-based model. What is referred to in this case is actually artificial sampling, where data values are generated with a computer from a known probability distribution, so that complex and otherwise intractable parameter estimates can be determined without expensive, perhaps even impossible, data collection.

The significant power for efficient allocation of resources in aid of narrative fulfillment represented by these rational protocols gives them superior positions in the pantheon of choice processes. It is this superior performance, historically incontrovertible, that suggests an ever-widening venue of application. But most humans cannot enlist the aid of these methods without extensive training and the assistance of a variety of other parties. Even as powerful as they are, they are bounded by the time and other resources required for their utilization in the face of the urgency and importance of the particular choice problem at hand. That is, they are examples of *bounded* rationality, in spite of what they may seem. Bounded rationality is almost always portrayed in contrast to the messianic alternative of the demonic methods noted by Gigerenzer. This "Laplacian Daemon" is the all-seeing, all-knowing supreme intelligence that can solve any resource allocation problem and select the globally best option for all individuals for all time. Fortunately, but beyond in the context of this discussion, it cannot exist.

All of the rational choice mechanisms mentioned above are available for the specification of agent choice protocols. All have computer programs that fully specify how they should be executed, what the data should look like, how the results should be presented and the limitations on and conditions of their application. Moreover, it is clear that a number of organizations and institutions make extensive use of these methods. Companies routinely use operations research for a variety of optimal resource allocation tasks. Perhaps one of the more interesting and successful applications of operations research is the revenue management process used in the sale of tickets in the airline industry, now being extended to similar perishable goods such as hotel rooms, rental cars, and theater seats.

But the individual human being does not routinely engage such mechanisms in making choices. In fact, as noted above, they are very likely to be reductive and not structural models, and therefore may describe no actual process found in real world. There is no evidence that human beings actually make routine choices using any of these tools. Humans tend to employ much simpler approaches to day-to-day choices, and in many instances extend these simple protocols to serious, far reaching and life-changing circumstances where the more sophisticated, rational methods would seem to be called for. Given that an agent model of the human decision-maker must describe what the modeled human actually does, and not what it could or should do, these less rigorous and more *ad hoc* choice protocols must also be made available to the human agent modeler.

5. An example: the AirMarkets simulator flight choice model

A specific example of an agent-based, rational choice model is the AirMarkets Simulator, which is a representation of the narrative structure and related choice protocol which portrays the behavior of customers selecting from a set of alternative air flight choices. Because the available flights at any point in time is partially a function of the choices made by others previously, a run of the simulation consists of all individuals (or groups traveling together) in the world traveling on commercial air service for a week's time period, with travel bookings starting 120 days before the subject week. (That time period insures that no flight is unavailable at any time before the 120-day booking period, so all individuals booking before the start can be done at once.) About 27 million travel individuals or parties are booked on each simulation run, making up about 42,000,000 individual customers.

Each travel party chooses from all available service connecting the desired origin to the desired destination. The alternative is chosen using a random number generator to produce a probability between 0 and 1, and then the probabilities associated with the available options are examined in arbitrary order to determine which is selected by that particular customer. The utility shown in Eq. (4) above has the following form for the value of $V(i, j)$, where i is the indicator of the customer and j the indicator of the air travel option:

$$\begin{aligned} V(i,j) = {} & \beta_f(i)\ln f(j) + d(j)[\beta_d(i) + \beta_{bd}(i)\ln d_{base}] \\ & + \beta_{dc}(i)N_{dc}(j) + \beta_{ic}(i)N_{ic}(j) \\ & + \beta_{1st}(i)X_{1st}(j) + \beta_{ec}(i)X_{ec}(j) + G(\tau(i) - t(j)) \end{aligned} \tag{6}$$

In this equation, the β's are coefficients that reflect the values carried by the traveler with index i associated with the of the flight option reflected by the attribute denoted by the j-value. For example, $\beta_{f(i)}$ is the value for traveler i with respect to the fare $f(j)$ associated with flight option j. Other important flight attributes include travel time, $d(j)$, the shortest flight time d_{base}, the number of stops in the flight that are associated with allied airlines $N_{dc}(j)$ and non-allied carriers $N_{ic}(j)$, and the cabin class of the flight option (first or economy). The β coefficients are estimated from extensive empirical data collected for that purpose.

The function $G(\tau(i) - t(j))$ is peculiar in the sense that it represents the desirability of the departure or arrival time of a flight option. (Note that either departure or arrival time is dominant, since the actual flight time cannot be altered by the traveler.) The passenger does not care if a flight takes off (or arrives) between two values a or b. If it is outside this range, then the further away from the a or b value, the less desirable the option is. The function G is referred to as a *Box-Cox* formulation, and is of the following form:

$$G(\tau(i) - t(j)) = \begin{cases} \beta_E(i)\dfrac{(t(j) - \tau(i) - a + 1)^{\lambda_E} - 1}{\lambda_E} & \tau(i) - t(j) < -a \\ 0 & -a < \tau(i) - t(j) < b \\ \beta_L(i)\dfrac{(\tau(i) - t(j) - b + 1)^{\lambda_L} - 1}{\lambda_L} & \tau(i) - t(j) > b \end{cases} \tag{7}$$

In this equation, $t(j)$ is the departure (arrival) time of flight option j, $\tau(i)$ is the *desired* departure (arrival) time by traveler i, $\beta_E(i)$ and $\beta_L(i)$ are coefficients associated with the traveler i if the departure (arrival) is early E or late L, and λ_E and λ_L are empirical values for the traveling population estimated from observed data.

If the G function expresses the cost to a traveler of not departing (or arriving) when desired, then the compliment to it is the preference structure in the travel population of the desired departure (arrival) times. This function is purely empirical, and is denoted by $\Theta(\tau)$, where τ is the desired departure (arrival) time. Then, in accordance with the probability function illustrated by Eq. (5), we can represent the probability that traveler i will select flight option j over the time period $[0, W]$ (nominally 1 week) is given by

$$p_i(j) = \int_0^W \frac{e^{V(i,j|\tau(i))}}{\sum_{k \in \Phi(m)} e^{V(i,k|\tau(i))}} d\Theta(\tau). \tag{8}$$

This gives us an idea of the nature of a rational narrative protocol of use in an agent-based model describing human behavior with a computer system. The data which characterizes the behavior of the 27 million traveling parties moving by air in a typical week around the world is a substantial, but not at all difficult to create or maintain. (It is, however, expensive. Over $2.5 million were spent collecting the data that represents the empirical values of appropriate traveler data.) The AirMarkets Simulator executes on an Intel 8-processor desktop computer in about 35 minutes, with no other activity being executed simultaneously. A complete, detailed description of the underlying structure of the Simulator is given in [3], pp. 156–269.

6. Heuristic choice protocols

The models of rational human behavior implicit in the realization in economic theory briefly described so far—*homo economicus*—are not the only kind of human choice that is, possible. In fact, there is scant evidence that people behave anything like the optimizing behavior suggested by these protocols. Virtually every scholar who examines the problem derides the idyllic nature of rational, economic humans. Indeed, the economic man model is often more normative than descriptive. While quite useful, as demonstrated by its singular success, applying a normative model ultimately begs the question of how people 'really' make choices, and to that extent the economic theory that is, the foundation of discrete choice and utility maximization methods is defective. And it is not necessary with the development of agent-based simulation models. The alternative to economic man is often couched somewhat inappropriately in terms of bounded rationality.

Bounded rationality refers to the limitations in resources available to undertake and perform data collection and analysis leading up to a decision, in other words, the execution of benefit/cost analyses, formal or otherwise. In this regard, two streams of thought are discernable in the analysis of human rational behavior. The one, stemming from game theory explores human decision making as a *real-valued trade-off* endeavor. Indeed, classic economic theory assumes that all the entities in a given economy converge to such utility function rationality as equilibrium is reached. Among the many tributaries of this line of thought is the utility structure that leads to discrete choice theory and the modern study of consumer choice behavior discussed previously. The second stream is the notion of *satisficing* as a decision structure. Satisficing is choice-making based on being "good enough" rather than "utility maximizing." This idea fits into the narrative framework.

Gigerenzer and Selten[30] captures this idea with a simple taxonomy of rational choice. Which he refers to as "visions of rationality." He breaks rationality down into two broad classes. One he calls *demons*, referring to the demonic capabilities he views as necessary to carry out rational decision-making in the real world without regard for constraints of time or resources, as mentioned. Demonic reasoning is dissected into *unbounded rationality* and *optimization under constraints*. The former is literally applying limitless resources to a decision problem or being presented with a decision problem so simple (such as a statistical estimation problem) that all relevant issues are easily known. The latter refers to concepts such as those frequently seen in operations research, in which the problem at hand has been constrained to become manageable. In this case, however, the choice of the nature and values of the constraints are subject to the same resource limitations as any decision problem, thus only begging the issue of what level of demonic strength is available. Gigerenzer suggests that the bounded rationality side consists of two components; the search for options or alternatives, encompassed under the label of "satisficing," and the actual choice among alternatives, referred to with the term "fast and frugal" heuristics. The searching activity includes methods for finding options and methods for stopping the search. Some of the search methods

Gigerenzer notes include: *random search*, where the agent explores the decision environment without any apparent organization until time runs out; *ordered search*, using the validity of environmental cues as they apply to the choice problem at hand as the ordering mechanism; search by *imitation* using apparent similarities of this decision problem to those encountered in the past (imitation allows us to know where to look and what to look for, but does limit results if the environment within which we are searching is novel or unexpected); and *emotions*, which apparently act to narrow down the search space in effective, but not well understood, ways. Other search methods readily come to mind, but all of them can be interpreted as being enabled by the narrative context in which the choice event is presented. That is, the search process is governed by what the agent, because of the controlling narrative that is, creating the decision context, considers important to the resource allocation and outcome probabilities associated with the atomic narrative.

Stopping the search is where satisficing comes in—when have we searched long enough and established enough options? When we are satisfied that further research will not add any important alternatives, or when we have no more time to gain additional knowledge? Gigerenzer [31], pp. 129–165, proposes what he calls the *probabilistic mental model* (PMM) as a construct to account for the satisficing and fast and frugal heuristic choice protocols. In a PMM, the individual puts the choice event in hand into a mental construct of similar choice situations it has encountered in the past, or has learned by one method or another, and uses that context as the satisficing criterion. In other words, people fit decision problems into models that seem somehow appropriate to the problem, make the decision, then modify the model if expected results are not realized. This approach argues that the limited cognitive and computational ability of humans mitigate against a purely analytic benefit/cost structure in favor of agile and adaptive, if less than optimal, heuristic decision rules.

Heuristic protocols are choice mechanisms that rely on relatively little information and rule-of-thumb thinking. There is strong evidence that much of the choice behavior of humans is of this variety, if for no other reason that bounds on available time for decision-making prohibit any other approach. For example, Malcolm Gladwell's discussion of virtually instantaneous human decision making in his book *Blink* [32] addresses this phenomenon. Todd [33] offers a simple listing of some of the more important fast and frugal heuristics:

- When choosing between two alternatives, one recognized and the other not, the *recognition heuristic* says choose the recognized one. The basis for this heuristic seems to be that recognized alternatives are apt to be more successful, and therefore more likely to be recognized, and thus to evaluate the remaining options using the second most important criterion. He proceeds this way, moving down the prioritized list of criteria, until only one alternative remains. If he gets through the choosing them is a better idea. Note that increased option search can reduce choice efficiency if more recognized options are added.

- In the *take the best* heuristic the agent selects the best alternative as measured by one single criterion (e.g., price). Other dimensions which characterize the issue in question are not considered at all. One can see how this fits neatly into the narrative framework if the criterion reflects a resource deemed supremely important for the realization of the narrative, as it becomes the dominant factor in the decision. And different agents may have different criteria for what constitutes "best."

- An extended form of the take-the-best heuristic (which in fact can be shown to actually be rational) is *lexicographic ordering*. This is a multi-dimensional extension of take-the-best. This line of thought has been explored more fully by Tversky [34] with his *elimination by aspects* approach. Elimination by aspects is a choice method wherein the individual has a set of criteria in mind on which he will evaluate a set of alternative choices. He ranks the criteria from most to least important, and then proceeds to evaluate each alternative against the first criterion. If two more alternatives have equal values according to that criterion, he eliminates all the others from consideration and moves on to the next criterion. If he reaches the last criterion evaluation and he has more than one choice alternative left, he selects among the remaining alternatives at random; that is, engages a random protocol. The phrase 'lexicographic' is also used to describe this protocol, since alphabetic ordering is done this way. Tversky also showed the equivalence of elimination by aspects to discrete choice thus moving this seeming heuristic into the domain of the rational.

- Another fast and frugal heuristic approach that lies on the boundary between pure rule of thumb and the rational choice operations is *Dawes's rule* [35]. This is a type of linear result choice method. Evaluate the alternatives against a set of criteria by determining if the alternative is either positive or negative with respect to each criterion and subtract the number of negatives from the number of positives. The option with the highest score is chosen.

- Other heuristics are described by scholars in several fields, especially cognitive psychology. Kunda [12] offers an extensive array. She mentions the *representative heuristic*, wherein a choice is based on the similarity of the choice situation a category of choices that have been faced or witnessed before (Kunda [12], pp. 57–89). The determination of similarity is based on characteristics of the situation at hand to the one or more of the attributes that define a class of situations but may differ from members of the class in details. This is conceptually coherent if viewed from a narrative perspective, in the sense that the value of resources and the weight put on the factors which assess that value that play in a narrative may be the among the criteria that define the class similarity. In this sense it is somewhat like the recognition heuristic described above.

- Another family of heuristic methods cited by Kunda is the collection of *statistical heuristics*, referring to statistical rules-of-thumb most people seem to have learned and carry around with them. They generally seem to arise as a result of dealing with the pervasive uncertainty life brings. For example, the observation that while having all nine of one's grandchildren be of the same gender would seem quite unusual to most people, having all three of your grandchildren would not seem that odd. But why? The suggestion is that people apply an elementary bit of statistics to the problem, reasoning that the gender of a child is a fifty-fifty proposition, and, equating that to the tosses of a coin, where tossing nine heads in a row happens much less often then than tossing three in a row.

- One final contribution to the heuristic array is more subtle than the others. This is *anchoring and adjustment* ([12] pp. 102–109). This is the tendency for people to base a decision about a specific issue based on a reference to other (perhaps completely irrelevant) situations. That is, some change in an element of the context in which the choice operation is taking place may cause a choice to vary from one instance to another, even though the context change is not part of the choice event. This setting of an anchor (the changing context element) will cause individuals to tend to adjust their choices to be consistent with the anchor, even though the anchor does not bear on the choice event itself.

There are many additional heuristic processes that could be identified, and this would seem to be a fertile area for further research. There is a considerable psychological and sociological literature that should be explored to extract current understanding of the choice mechanisms and formulate computing structures that would be applicable to agent-based models. There is little doubt these mechanisms are used very frequently in many day-to-day choice situations and they should be available to the human agent modeler as much as the more flamboyant rational methods are. But in their implementation their sometime severe bias must also be recognized. That is, just as much a part of the protocol as the actual choice itself.

7. Social network choice protocols

Humans rarely make decisions completely alone. Many choices are subject to consideration and examination by not only the chooser directly, but also by other individuals who are connected to her in some way. Friends, relatives, other respected (or not so respected) experts, celebrities, people in authority, co-workers and many others enter into the choice making process in a host of ways, and with a variety of consequences. Only a few of such mechanisms can be considered here.

In a sense, social network choice protocols are somewhere between the rational approaches and the individual heuristics. Gigerenzer poses the dilemma:

> "In many real-world situations, there are multiple pieces of information, which are not independent, but redundant. Here Bayes' rule and other 'rational' algorithms quickly become mathematically intractable, at least for ordinary human minds.[6] These situations make neither of these two views [laws of probability, and reasoning error] look promising. If one was to apply the classical view to complex, real-world environments, this would suggest that the mind is a supercalculator—carrying around the collected works of Kolmogoroff, Fisher and Neyman—and simply needs a memory jog .... On the other hand, the heuristics and biases view of human irrationality would lead us to believe that humans are hopelessly lost in the face of real-world complexity, given their supposed inability to reason according to the canon of classical rationality, even in simple laboratory experiments." ([31], pp. 167)

That most people survive without falling into Gigerenzer's abyss is due in part to social network choice methods. Clark [36] makes a compelling argument in support of this vital role, suggesting that the "scaffolding" of the social network in which all humans are embedded is central to our ability to make decisions, survive and advance. Kunda provides a broad but insightful survey of the field, and Sternberg and Ben-Zeev [37] offer an excellent introduction. The rapid rise of social networking sites on the internet—Facebook, Twitter—testify to both the importance of the social network and the ease with which people adapt to new forms of it.

The development of formal methods of social network analysis has become quite active, as well, partly because of the advances in computing and agent-based

[6] It is easy to create a simple example where Bayesian analysis generates formulations which are not only mentally intractable, but mathematically intractable as well. Consider virtually any non-trivial situation where there is no conjugate prior.

modeling. Network analysis as a formal field of academic endeavor dates back at least to Erdos and Renyi [38] but the emergence of the worldwide web has spurred more recent advances, including the exploration of scale free and stochastic network analysis. An easily accessible introductory survey of modern methods can be found in Barabasi [39] or Buchanan [40]. A more advanced and formal treatment is offered by Dorogovtsev and Mendes [41]. Newman et al., [42] have compiled a compendium of more recent developments in the field.

In an agent-based modeling context, networks are an expression of the topology of the explicit space required by Epstein's definition of agent model (Epstein [28]). That is, a network defines which agent is "close to" which other agent. Moreover, it defines what the word "close" means in a particular model. Epstein and Axtell illustrate the network role on the *Sugerscape* grid with respect to economic and social interaction ([43], pp. 130–135). As they show, a network in an agent-based model is a communication connection between one agent and another. A single agent can have such connections with a number of other agents. The connection can be one-way or two-way. Different kinds of connections can reflect differences in the nature of the inter-agent communication. And, perhaps more importantly, networks change over time, with new connections being made and older ones dying out.

A convenient way to consider the network structure of an agent-based model is to stipulate that each agent will maintain a list of the other agents to whom it is connected. Separate lists can be kept for different kinds of communications. If two agents have each other in their individual lists, then the network communication link is mutual, otherwise it is just one way. The *message posting* function of the computer implementation of an agent model can then be engaged to manage the communications between agents during the simulation. However, network structures are not a requirement of an agent model. Space can be portrayed in other ways. In a cellular automaton, agents reside on a grid where communications between agents is based on being physically next to each other on the grid. In the AirMarkets Simulator, simple agent communication networks are used to define the relationships between distribution system agents and airline agents.

Perhaps the most common form of social network-dictated choice protocol is *imitation*. There is strong evidence human beings learn by imitation, and thus it is reasonable that the same approach would be called on when faced with a new choice situation. What action did others do in this same situation? Very often the narrative event which creates the choice is encountered in the context of a shared narrative, and thus the choice by the individual is apt to follow the course of the underlying narrative supporting the event definition. In terms of agent-modeling, the agent which uses this protocol must be linked through a social network to the individual or group of individuals whom it wants to imitate. The imitation cannot be certain, however, for that is, reserved for consilvocation. There must be a randomizing mechanism that allows for the imitation to have a stochastic element, such as being linked to two or more individuals who can be imitated, but with a randomization device that dictates which one is followed in a particular event.

Closely related to imitation is *expert advice*. It is natural that someone believed to know more about a particular narrative event—an expert in the field—would make a wiser choice than a novice. And as humans learn as children and adolescents, the courses of action suggested by experts with more experience are important techniques in determining the probability of the outcomes of various choice options. From an agent modeling perspective, clearly a social network link is needed between the agent and the expert. Again, some stochastic mechanism needs to be present if the requirements of the narrative construct are going to be met. In this case, however, in addition to the selection of one of a possible set of experts, whether or not to follow the expert advice can be employed as the randomization method. Taleb ([44], pp. 145–156) examines what he refers to as the "expert problem" in some depth, classifying experts into those who have expertise in subjects for which expertise exists, such as science and medicine, and reserves the phrase "empty suits" for those who claim expertise in things for which no expertise can possibly exist, such as the forecasting the value of a stock exchange index tomorrow morning.

This raises an issue to be addressed by an agent model that uses either imitation or reference to experts: How do those experts make a decision which can be imitated or on which expert opinion can be founded? One might suggest that the "imitand" or the expert use a rational choice method, for example. Or there could be hierarchies of imitators or experts, each imitating others while providing expertise to other agents. It would be quite interesting to explore how such networks might work with a simple agent model. In particular, emergent properties of agent-based simulations which contain such social mechanisms could be most curious. Finally, note that the required stochastic property of the choice process of an agent using imitation or experts could be inherited from the stochastic property of the imitated or expert agents.

A third kind of social network choice protocol is *voting*. An individual can make a choice by polling a set of other individuals to see what they would choose, and then determine his or her choice by tallying the results. For a simple binary choice, this technique is trivial. (Again, how those who cast votes determined their respective choices is a modeling design issue.) For choice events where three or more options and three or more individuals are polled, however, Kenneth Arrow's Impossibility Theorem enters the picture, and some form of bias has to be introduced to guarantee an outcome [45]. Again, implementation of this type of social network decision protocol is straightforward in the design of an agent-based model. The agent in question maintains a list of voters and polls each one by supplying the voter with the choice problem and accepting that voter's choice as the vote. The agent then tallies the votes and determines its choice.

A particularly strong form of social choice is not extensively discussed in the literature, at least as far as he research of this author has been able to find. The concept has been termed by associates as *consilvocation*.[7] In this situation, an agent turns over to another agent complete control over the choice to be made. A trivial example is the husband leaving to the wife the choice of restaurant for dinner. Consilvocation happens all the time in a democratic political context. The individual citizen elects a representative to sit in a legislative body and make decisions on his behalf. The citizen has thus turned over the choice function to the representative.

Consilvocation is a way of eliminating choice events that are out of an individual's control but will have an impact on the course of a compound narrative. It simplifies matters considerably. Another attribute of the consilvocation choice protocol is that the consilvocated right to make the decision can be revoked. The process by which revocation occurs can be simple (the husband elects to pick the restaurant himself) or complex (the citizen must wait for the next election or invoke a recall process). Adding consilvocation to an agent model is generally not difficult but could well have a dramatic impact on the number of individuals demonstrating a specific behavior in relatively a large-scale agent model simulation.

---

[7] This term was coined by a colleague who graduated from Oxford and has a sharp interest in the English language. He was assisted—although he did not know it—by a friend whose command of English is also admirable, and American. The American refined the Oxford graduate's original construction, which was virtually unpronounceable.

Recall that in the AirMarkets Simulator, a single agent actually represents multiple passengers, and one agent buys tickets for everyone in the group it represents.

8. Bias in choice

Finally, the term *bias* in the context of this analysis refers to the difference between the choice that is, actually made and the choice that would be made if the "correct" alternative were selected. Obviously, this calls for a definition of "correct." In a formal statistical decision problem, bias refers to the difference between the expectation of a particular statistic that is, used to estimate the parameter and the value of the estimate itself. That is, a statistic S used to estimate a parameter θ is *unbiased* if $E[S] = \theta$, and the search for unbiased estimators is a long-standing topic of statistical research. The definition of correct is not so easily determined in the agent choice circumstance.

Many authors identify and describe choice bias in a manner similar to the statistical definition, holding that the choice that results from the engagement of a rational decision protocol is the correct one, and other heuristic or social network protocols that lead to different choices for the same narrative event are biased. As has been said before, if human beings are to be validly represented by agent-based models, then they must be represented as they are, not how someone thinks they ought to be.[8]

Some biases are perceptual in nature, and arise from inaccurate representations of reality, which in terms of the formal definition of agent can be accommodated with properties of the perceptor component. Festinger et al. [46] and Tumminia [47] explore some of the implication of cognitive dissonance, which occurs when an individual believes in a reality that is, directly contradicted by the sensory evidence before him. The *mistakes-were-made* assertion described by Shermer [8], pp. 67–71 is an example of *self-justification* bias [48]. *Inattentional blindness* is the failure to recognize some feature of the surrounding environment because attention is focused on some other environmental feature [49]. *Blind spot bias* is the ability to see biased perception on the part of others but fail to see it in oneself. It is similar to *better-than-average* bias, which causes a person to think they are more capable at any given skill or talent than the average individual [50]. Humans also tend to see themselves in a more positive light than they see others [51], and therefore create a *self-serving bias*. People tend to accept credit when they behave in socially acceptable ways and blame circumstances outside themselves when they do not do so well. This is an example of an *attribution bias* [52].

But not all biases are perceptual. Two, in particular, are based on misunderstanding fundamental concepts in probability theory. Kunda ([12], pp. 54–62) notes that probability theory, as a formal mathematical discipline, dates only back 300 years,[9] and that its relatively late development speaks to its intuitive difficulty. One is the *base rate bias*, described nicely by Kunda, and the other is the so-called *Let us Make A Deal* fallacy, described by Shermer ([8] pp. 83–84). Base rate bias is very common. It stems from misunderstanding the incidence of some particular characteristic in the underlying population, and thus from a miss-application of Bayes' Rule to an intuitive inference. For example, consider John, who is a small gentleman with a quiet demeanor, who wears glasses, dresses conservatively, and

[8] However, there are potentially some interesting agent-based models to be built that explore the effects of the biased choice protocol versus the rational on the outcome of a narrative.

[9] She's wrong, in one respect. Formal probability theory, where probability is defined in terms of normed measure spaces, dates back only 85 years or so.

often is seen carrying a book. Is John a factory worker or a librarian? Many would say a librarian. But the likelihood that he is a factory worker is far higher than he is a librarian. None of the distinguishing criteria disqualifies him from being a factory worker, and there are far more factory workers than librarians. This is the base rate fallacy; failing to account for the actual rate of incidence of a factor in making a judgment. It is a primary reason for bias in the representative heuristic.

The Let us-Make-a-Deal fallacy is significantly more subtle. The name refers to a game show popular on American daytime television. A contestant stands before three closed doors, behind one of which is a valuable prize, usually a car. Behind the other two are valueless prizes, historically goats (but animal rights advocates objected, so some other worthless offering is now used). Which door hides which prize is unknown to the contestant. The contestant chooses one of the doors and is awarded the prize behind that door, hopefully the car. But before the chosen door is opened, the host opens one of the other two doors (always revealing a goat) and asks the contestant if she wants to change her door choice and take the prize behind the remaining door. Should the contestant take the offer, or should she stay with her original selection? Most people will say it does not matter. Assuming that the likelihood of a car being behind any of the three doors is the same (one third) for each, then knowing that it is not behind one of them only means that the probability of it being behind either of the remaining two is now changed to one half, and therefore switching does not affect the odds of winning. But that is, incorrect. In fact, the probability that the car is behind the door that was chosen originally by the contestant is one third, and that it is behind the unrevealed other door is two thirds.[10] The explanation is clear (but for many, not convincing). The contestant faces three possibilities: the doors can hide (1) car, goat, goat; (2) goat, car, goat; or (3) goat, goat, car. Suppose she starts the game by selecting door number one. Then if she switches and the first possibility is the true situation, she loses. But if either of the other two possibilities are the case and she switches, she wins. Thus, the probability of winning by switching is two thirds. A simple computer application is easy to write that simulates the game any desired number of times. Execution of that simulation verifies the correctness of the analysis.

There are, of course, many similar examples of incorrect reasoning. That they exist and should be avoided in the making of careful decisions is obvious. But it is equally obvious that these "errors" can be subtle, and difficult to detect. Once again, human agents in computer simulations must be modeled as they are, not as they should be. That means determining when bias is an important part of the agent behavior and building that bias into the agent. But as difficult as the task might seem initially, it is ameliorated by the knowledge that choice protocols span cultures and societies, so what is learned on one context can be applied in others, and, with the connection of the choice protocol to the narrative framework, complex behaviors can be built up out of simpler, atomic elements.

9. Conclusions

This presentation sets the stage for more exhaustive incorporation of narrative structures into human behavior-based computer artificial intelligence applications.

---

[10] This puzzle was first presented by the columnist Marilyn vos Savant in a U.S. national Sunday newspaper supplement a few years ago. When she explained how the probability of winning went to 2/3 if the other door were selected, a firestorm of protest erupted from the academic statistics world. She is right, however.

One such application has been in operation for the last several years in the AirMarkets Corporation, consisting of an agent-based model of air passenger behavior, including flight schedule development, revenue management of air fares as a function of advanced booking time, departure and arrival times, group size and available service. Because of the interdependency of air fares, available service and air demand, for each run the AirMarkets Simulation replicates the air travel utilization for every seat on every scheduled flight taking place in the world for a week time period. That is, more than 42,000,000 passengers buying tickets in approximately 288,000 directional city-pair markets over a single week time period, with advanced booking being as much as 120 days in advance of departure. The narrative structure supporting this agent-based simulation is not complex. Since travel is usually a utility associated with some other activity, a choice function based on the utility value of departure/arrival times, fares, booking times and travel purpose is sufficient for the AirMarkets Simulation. Other behavior activities, however, will require more in-depth structuring.

Beyond the semi-rational construction of narratives using hard logic and mathematics, the description of human narrative decision-making gets much softer and more obscure. The heuristic thinking by individuals is perhaps rational, perhaps not. It depends on how accurate the time-dependent, context-constricted thinking of the decision-maker turns out to be. In a logically-looser setting, social structure can become the basis for narrative behavior and the guidelines for assessing the validity of the option choices become even less rigorous. Finally, there is a substantial level of human narrative activity that can only be classified as bias. There is no logic, no bounded rationality and no social context which explains such narrative behavior. In this area several frivolous, and several dangerous, actions by human narrative holders are justified.

However, there is one pressing issue among the several that exist must be addressed. It is necessary to explore the impacts of at least four mathematical anomalies on the structure of even a simple, atomic narrative. These are: (1) the Stone-Weierstrass Theorem, which stipulates the minimum mathematical structure for a data set contents to be represented by a polynomial (which in turn can become part of a narrative, but might not be consistent across several data sets); (2) the Arrow Impossibility Theorem, which shows the theoretical limits of rational decision-making on electoral processes; (3) Godel's Theorem, which determines that any logical structure is subject to questions about completeness that can only be addressed using a logical structure more in question than the one being assessed; and (4) the Heisenberg Uncertainty Principle, which cites limits on observable, non-probabilistic statements of the physical universe. The exploration of these issues are the subject of my current research.

Author details

Roger Parker
AirMarkets Corporation, Edmonds, WA, USA

*Address all correspondence to: rap@airmarkets.aero

References

[1] Parker R. The construction of agent simulations of human behavior. In: Karwowski W, Abram T, editors. Intelligent Human Systems Integration, Proceedings of the 2nd IHSI Conference: Integrating People and Intelligent Systems 903. Springer; 2019. pp. 435-441

[2] Parker R. The AirMarkets simulation program. In: Everett WA, editor. PNW AIAA Conference; 2014

[3] Parker R. Virtual markets: The application of agent-based modeling to marketing science [dissertation]. Sydney, Australia: University of Technology; 2010

[4] Montague R. Your Brain is (Almost) Perfect. New York, NY: Plume; 2006. pp. 69-72

[5] Danto A. Narrative and Knowledge. New York, NY: Columbia University Press; 1985

[6] Fisher W. Human Communication as Narrative: Toward a Philosophy of Reason, Value and Action. Columbia, SC: University of South Carolina Press; 1987

[7] Sober E, Wilson D. Unto Others: The Evolution and Psychology of Unselfish Behavior. Cambridge, MA: Harvard University Press; 1998

[8] Shermer M. The Mind of the Market. New York, NY: Henry Holt & Co.; 2008

[9] Popper K. The Logic of Scientific Discovery. London, UK: Routledge; 2002. pp. 79-82

[10] Parker R, Bakken D. Predicting the unpredictable: Agent-based models for market research. In: Mouncey P, Wimmer F, editors. Best Practice in Market Research. New York, NY: John Wiley and Sons; 2007

[11] Parker R, Perroud D. Exploring markets with agent-based computer simulations. In: 60th Annual ESOMAR Congress; Montreal Canada. 2008

[12] Kunda Z. Social Cognition. Cambridge, MA: MIT Press; 1999

[13] Gilbert N, Troitzsch K. Simulation for the Social Scientist. Milton Keynes, UK: Open University Press; 1999

[14] Axelrod R. The Complexity of Cooperation: Agent-Based Models of Competition and Collaboration. Princeton, NJ: Princeton University Press; 1997

[15] Wooldridge M. An Introduction to MultiAgent Systems. New York, NY: John Wiley and Sons; 2002

[16] Jackson D. Fourier Analysis and Orthogonal Polynomials. Oberlin OH; Casus; Mathematical Monographs; Mathematical Association of America; 1941

[17] Grenander U, Rosenblatt M. Statistical Analysis of Stationary Time Series. New York, NY: John Wiley and Sons; 1952

[18] Ben-Akiva M, Lerman S. Discrete Choice Theory. Cambridge, MA: MIT Press; 1985

[19] Louviere J, Hensher P, Swait J. Stated Choice Methods. Cambridge, UK: Cambridge University Press; 2000

[20] Cox D, Oakes D. Analysis of Survival Data. London, UK: Chapman and Hall; 1984

[21] Hewitt E, Stromberg K. Real and Abstract Analysis. Heidelberg, DE: Springer-Verlag; 1965. pp. 94-98

[22] Auffhammer M, Carson R. Forecasting the path of China's CO_2

emissions using province-level information. Journal of Environmental Economics and Management. 2008; **55**(3):229-247. DOI: 10.1016/j.jeem.2007.10.002

[23] Parker R, Cenesizoglu T, Carson R. Aggregation Issues in Forecasting Aggregate Demand: An Application to U.S. Commercial Air Travel, Advanced Research Techniques Forum. Couer d'Alene ID: American Marketing Association; 2005

[24] Chang C, Keisler H. Model Theory. Amsterdam, NL, North Holland: Elsevier; 1973

[25] Humphreys P. Extending Ourselves: Computational Science, Empiricism, and Scientific Method. Cambridge, UK: Oxford University Press; 2004. pp. 108-109

[26] UIUC. Guide to the Human Relations Area Files. University of Illinois at Urbana-Champaign; 2009

[27] Brown D. Human Universals. New York, NY: McGraw-Hill; 1991

[28] Epstein J. Generative Social Science: Studies in Agent-Based Computational Modeling. Princeton, NJ: Princeton University Press; 2006

[29] Ferguson T. Mathematical Statistics: A Decision Theoretic Approach. San Diego, CA: Academic Press; 1967

[30] Gigerenzer G, Selten R. Bounded Rationality: The Adaptive Toolbox. Cambridge, MA: MIT Press; 2001

[31] Gigerenzer G. Adaptive Thinking: Rationality in the Real World. Cambridge, UK: Oxford University Press; 2000

[32] Gladwell M. Blink. Boston, MA: Little Brown and Company; 2005

[33] Todd P. Fast and frugal heuristics for environmentally bounded minds. In: Gigerenzer G, Selten R, editors. Bounded Rationality: The Adaptive Toolbox. Cambridge, MA: MIT Press; 2001

[34] Tversky A. Elimination by aspects: A theory of choice. Psychology Review. 1972;**79**:281-299

[35] Dawes R. The robust beauty of improper linear methods in decision making. American Psychology. 1979;**34**: 571-582

[36] Clark A. Being There: Putting Brain, Body and World Together Again. Cambridge, MA: MIT Press; 1997

[37] Sternberg R, Ben-Zeev T. Complex Cognition: The Psychology of Human Thought. Cambridge, UK: Oxford University Press; 2001

[38] Erdos P, Renyi A. On the evolution of random graphs. In: Newman M, Barabasi A, Watts D, editors. The Structure and Dynamics of Networks. Princeton, NJ: Princeton University Press; 1960

[39] Barabasi A. Linked: The New Science of Networks. New York, NY: Perseus; 2002

[40] Buchanan M. Small Worlds and the Groundbreaking Theory of Networks. New York, NY: W.W. Norton and Co; 2002

[41] Dorogovtsev S, Mendes J. Evolution of Networks: From Biological Nets to the Internet and WWW. Cambridge, UK: Oxford University Press; 2003

[42] Newman M, Barabasi A-L, Watts D. The Structure and Dynamics of Networks. Princeton, NJ: Princeton University Press; 2008

[43] Epstein J, Axtell R. Growing Artificial Societies: Social Sciences from

the Bottom Up. Cambridge, MA: The MIT Press; 1996. pp. 130-135

[44] Taleb N. The Black Swan. London, UK: Random House; 2007

[45] Arrow K. Social Choice and Individual Values. 2nd ed. New Haven, CT: Yale University Press; 1963

[46] Festinger L, Rieckin H, Schachter S. Where Prophecy Fails: A Social and Psychological Study. New York, NY: HarperCollins; 1964

[47] Tumminia D. When Prophecy Never Fails: Myth and Reality in a Flying-Saucer Group. Cambridge, UK: Oxford University Press; 2006

[48] Tarvis C, Aronson E. Mistakes Were Made (but Not by Me). San Diego, CA: Harcourt; 2007

[49] Simons D, Chabris C. Gorillas in our midst: sustained inattentional blindness for dynamic events. Perception. 1999; **28**:1059-1074

[50] Pronin E, Gilovich T, Ross L. Objectivity in the eye of the beholder: Divergent perceptions of bias in self versus others. Psychology Review. 2004;**111**:781-799

[51] Kruger J. Personal beliefs and cultural stereotypes about racial characteristics. Journal of Personality and Social Psychology. 1996;**71**:536-548

[52] Nesbitt R, Ross L. Human Inference, Strategies and Shortcomings of Social Judgment. Upper Saddle River, NJ: Prentice-Hall; 1980

Chapter 7

SAML-QC: A Stochastic Assessment and Machine Learning-Based QC Technique for Industrial Printing

Azhar Hussain and Kamal Bhattarai

Abstract

Recently, the advancement in industrial automation and high-speed printing has raised numerous challenges related to the printing quality inspection of final products. This chapter proposes a machine vision-based technique to assess the printing quality of text on industrial objects. The assessment is based on three quality defects such as text misalignment, varying printing shades, and misprinted text. The proposed scheme performs the quality inspection through stochastic assessment technique based on the second-order statistics of printing. First, the text-containing area on a printed product is identified through image processing techniques. Second, the alignment testing of the identified text-containing area is performed. Third, optical character recognition is performed to divide the text into different small boxes, and only the intensity value of each text-containing box is taken as a random variable, and second-order statistics are estimated to determine the different printing defects in the text under one, two, and three sigma thresholds. Fourth, the k-nearest neighbors (k-NN)-based supervised machine learning is performed to provide the stochastic process for misprinted text detection. Finally, the technique is deployed on an industrial image for the printing quality assessment with varying values of n and m. The results have shown that the proposed SAML-QC technique can perform real-time automated inspection for industrial printing.

Keywords: stochastic assessment, machine learning, k-NN, printing quality, automation

1. Introduction

The quality control and inspection of the high-speed printing process is a critical topic in various industries ranging from electronics to pharmaceutical products. The advent of higher quality requirements from end users and higher costs of raw materials has limited the profit margin of labeling producers. The label producers need to improve the quality of their products and improve the production efficiency by keeping the cost and management thresholds to a minimum level. Typical industrial label printing mechanisms include offset-printing, letterpress-printing, combination-printing, and flexography printing. Various challenges faced by the labels are the limited sized of text-containing region, relatively small size of labels, clear text, ink-flow control for same shades, and text alignment. Usually, the common defects encountered in the printing process are misprinting, text fading, and various shades in printed text. According to the report [1], in 2010 the Chinese pharmaceutical label market demand was more than 165 million m^2, and the increase is predicted to be 10–12% in the next 3–5 years. Europe and America had a market demand of 300 million m^2 and 250 million m^2, respectively, and both are expected to increase by about 3% annually. It is evident that the market demand of pharmaceutical labels in western countries is higher than in China.

The Chinese market is expected to witness an increase in demand in the coming years. It is also reported that in the past 3 years, the labor costs have increased dramatically and QC management has become more difficult. Manual QC inspection can be easily affected by factors such as lack of experience, emotions, human eye perception, and environmental conditions. These factors lead to an inconsistent and poor standard of inspection. Although a review process is usually added in the inspection process in order to recheck the misprinted labels and quality defects, it cannot guarantee 100% quality inspection and also leads to extra labor costs and time consumption. In order to win the customer satisfaction, the inspection QC should be improved through automation. Even tiny mistakes in the label printing can put a bad impression in the overall product quality and can reduce a good customer relationship. Therefore, automatic inspection system is an obvious choice for the industries, and it will have room to grow in the near future.

The proposed scheme performs quality inspection in three steps. The first step is related to the inspection of printed text alignment with respect to the industrial object. Although the requirement for printing alignment is company specific, the proposed mechanism is adaptable and adjustable according to the specific requirement. The second step performs quality inspection based on detection of varying printing shades in the detected text. The third step is aided by supervised machine learning, and it performs the detection of misprinted text. The rest of the paper is composed as follows. Section 2 addresses the related work for computer-aided quality inspection of printing. Section 3 explains the SAML-QC algorithm. Section 4 shows the results of performing the proposed inspection on a given industrial object. Finally, Section 5 presents conclusion and future work.

2. Related works

Recently, a few researches have investigated computer-aided detection and image quality assessment. In [2] a technique based on the comparison of an inspected document with its referential version is discussed. In [3] an image quality assessment algorithm is proposed that does not rely on reference images, and its general framework emulates human quality assessment by first detecting visual components and then assessing quality against an empirical model for face detection. In the algorithm of Rowley et al. [4], a neural network is trained to detect face patterns in a region of 20-by-20 pixels. The determination of an arbitrary image such that if the square is a face region, the square is down-sampled to the size of 20 by 20 and equalized, resulting in a normalized signal.

A similar proposition holds for the face detector of Viola and Jones [5]. In their algorithm a feature-based classifier is trained over a square box of 24-by-24 pixels, with each feature defined by a feature template composed of a group of rectangular sub-windows. In [6], two machine learning algorithms are used for feature selection: mixture of Gaussian and radial basis function (RBF). The first one is a statistical distribution estimation-based algorithm, while the second is a function approximation-based algorithm. However, the preliminary experiment based only on face detection and face-based quality modeling yielded encouraging results. However, more work needs to be done in the areas such as object detection, feature selection, and machine learning to better establish this method.

As an efficient alternative, the machine vision systems can filter out the physical limitations and subjective judgmental decisions of humans. In [7] an image processing technique for the development of a low-cost machine vision system is explored for the inspection of the pharmaceutical capsule. This work discusses the two-part gelatin capsule inspection system by using image processing techniques for border tracing and approximation of the capsule to a circle. A quality control feedback performs pass/reject decision and puts capsules to the appropriate bin. In [8] a new approach for detecting the printing accuracy based on the technology of machine vision is presented.

The process consists of image acquisition, filtering, segmentation, and image matching. In this chapter, JSEG [9] algorithm is used to segment the textile printing images with obvious texture and then make a match for the segmented edge information, to obtain deviation area of the image and calculate the deviation position. However, in their experiments, several limitations are found for the system. One case is when the similar colors between the two neighbor regions cannot be segmented. The work in [10] introduced the algorithm based on wavelet packet and the regional analysis. It analyzes the significance of the threshold of binarization in defect detection combined with morphology area analysis method to extract specific features of defects and determine the type of defect. In [11] a study was conducted to evaluate how accurately a machine learning method can predict human judgment about printed pattern quality. Similarly [12] also proposed machine learning-based quality assessment scheme.

3. Proposed SAML-QC scheme

The block diagram of the proposed scheme is shown in **Figure 1**. It shows that the algorithm receives the input image and performs pre-filtering. The pre-filtering process starts by RGB to gray scale conversion and resizing the input image to a width of 500 pixels without losing the aspect ratio. A Gaussian blur (of kernel size 9×11) filters the salt and pepper noise in the image. Then the histogram

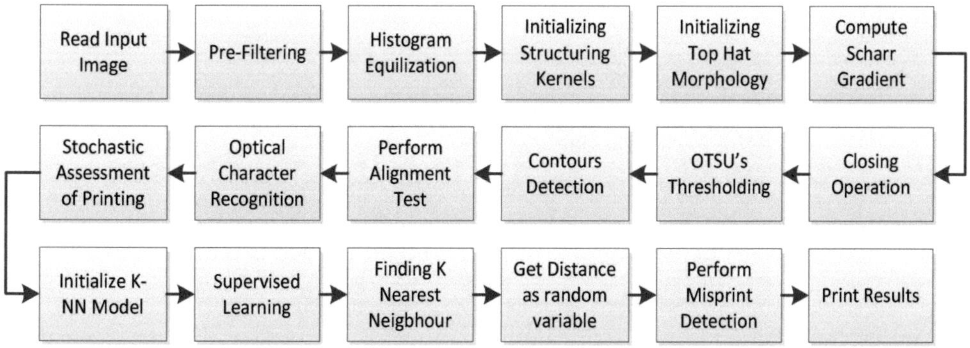

Figure 1.
Block diagram of SAML-QC algorithm.

equalization process enhances the contrast. The next step is the initialization of structuring kernels. These kernels play a major role in the morphological closing operation. This operation combines the text-containing region and supports the detection of text-containing region for the alignment testing. The next step is the initialization of TopHat morphology [13] to find the white regions against the darker ones.

It follows the computation of Scharr gradient [14] of the TopHat image for edge detection. The proposed scheme used the Sobel operator in horizontal axis to calculate the absolute value element-wise. The minimum and maximum values of Scharr gradient are obtained followed by scaling to the range 0–255 per pixel value. The next step performs the morphological closing operation to fill the gaps. It is followed by Otsu's auto-thresholding [15] to binaries the image. The morphological closing and dilation process is performed to convert the text-containing region as a combined blob. It is intuitive that this combined block contains the actual area of the text and makes the image ready for the detection of contours. The purpose of finding contours in the image is to detect the text-containing region inside the given object. After that, the text-containing region is cropped and stored in a buffer for later use in stochastic assessment. The text-containing region is identified by selecting the bounding box with optimum aspect ratio in the process of iterating over the found contours. The red rectangle is displayed on the image of the selected text. The coordinates of the text-containing region are used for the testing of text alignment.

3.1 Text alignment assessment

In printing industry the common text alignment errors are related to the horizontal and vertical alignments. In the current paper, it is assumed that the best position of the text is right at the center of the object. Therefore, any text region that is printed too much horizontally or vertically should be identified. However, the height and width of the industrial objects and their respective printed texts are different due to the varying nature of performance of the printing labelers as discussed in [10]. Therefore, the proposed algorithm presents a mathematical formulation to detect alignment error of the text inside an industrial object. **Figure 2** shows an abstract image of an industrial object (red portion) with markers showing the dimensions. The width and height of the industrial object are represented by Wo and Ho, respectively. The width and height of text-containing region are represented by w and h. Let (xo,yo) and (xt,yt) represent the top left corners for the object and text boxes, respectively, as shown in **Figure 2**. The absolute

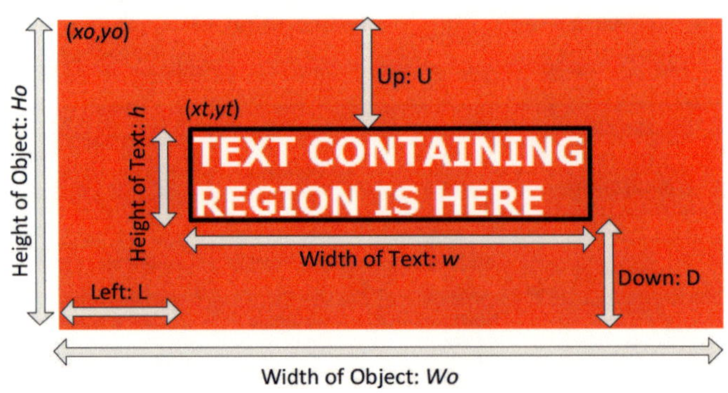

Figure 2.
Parameters for the alignment test of text-containing region.

difference in terms of pixels between the top edge of industrial object and top of the bounding box of the text region is given by Eq. (1), and similarly, the absolute differences for down and left are given by Eqs. (2) and (3):

$$U = abs\{(yo - yt)\} \tag{1}$$

$$D = abs\{(yo + Ho) - (yt + h)\} \tag{2}$$

$$L = abs\{(xo - xt)\} \tag{3}$$

The proposed criterion for text alignment is based on threshold value for vertical and horizontal alignments. Let UDThresh represent threshold for up-down or vertical alignment testing. The value of UDThresh is set as h. Let LThresh represent the left-right or horizontal alignment.

The value of LThresh is set as Wo/4. It means that it contains the width of one-fourth of the full width of object. The decision boundaries for horizontal and vertical alignment passed or failed are given as follows. If abs{(U-D)} ≤ UDThresh, then the vertical alignment is considered as passed else it is failed. If L ≤ LThresh, then the horizontal alignment is considered as passed, else it is considered as failed.

3.2 Optical character recognition

After the assessment of alignment, the next step is to perform the optical character recognition. For this purpose the proposed scheme crops the text-containing region ($xt, yt, x + h, w + h$) of the input image. The median filter is applied to remove any salt paper noise in the image. The next step is to perform the Gaussian blur with emphasis in the vertical direction by selecting the kernel size of 1×5. The reason behind this step is to exploit the nature of text printing. For example, in **Figure 2** the vertical difference between the TEXT CONTAINING and REGION IS HERE is more than the horizontal difference between consecutive individual letters. The next step in the process of obtaining optimum image ready to perform optical character recognition (OCR) is to perform the image contrast enhancement.

The proposed scheme used bilateral filtering [16] to improve the text regions while suppressing the background. The bilateral filtering alters the intensity value of each pixel with the weighted average of its neighbors that is Gaussian distributed. The next step is to perform the gray scale conversion and perform Otsu's autothresholding and bit-wise logical NOT operation to obtain binary image. This image is saved as a PNG format. This PNG image is provided as input image to the state-of-the-art Tesseract open-source OCR engine v3.02 [17]. The purpose of performing OCR is to get bounding boxes and location of anything that looks like a character. As a result an html file containing the position and sizes of each detected letter is generated. **Figure 3(a)** and **(b)** shows an image that is cropped

Figure 3.
The detection of bounding boxes of letters: (a) text area selected; and (b) detection of letters.

and processed by the stated procedure to get the detected boxes of letters in the text and marked with green rectangles.

3.3 Stochastic assessment of printing quality

The next block performs the stochastic assessment of the printing quality in terms of detection of overly faded printed text due to the imperfections in printing process as discussed in [1].

3.3.1 Detection of printing in varying shades

The intensity value of each printed pixel can be considered as a random variable *H* sampled at time *t*, and since its distribution is also unknown, therefore, it follows Gaussian distribution. From [18] it is clear that a sequence of random variables is independent and identically distributed (IID), if every random variable has the identical probability distribution and all are mutually independent. Thus it is also assumed that H is IID Gaussian random variable. The noise related to the intensity variation is Gaussian in nature; hence the mean and the acquired image also have additive Gaussian noise ni with H. In order to estimate the parameter H, from parametric space to the estimation space H′ via observation space y(H,t) at any time t, the maximum a posteriori probability (MAP) estimation [19] is used. MAP maximizes the a posteriori probability, which means most likely the value of H is given by Eq. (4):

$$\max_{\{H\}} f(H|y) = \max_{\{H\}} \left\{ \frac{f(y|H)f(H)}{f(y)} \right\} \tag{4}$$

It is quite clear that the probability density function (p.d.f) of parameter H needs to be determined in order to maximize the expression Eq. (4). It is assumed that ni is IID with *N* (0, σn2) and H is independent of ni with *N* (0, σH2). Let K be numbers of pixels which are available for a given box to estimate H. The conditional p.d.f of y given H is given by Eq. (5):

$$f(y|H) = \prod_{i=1}^{K} \frac{1}{\sqrt{2\pi\sigma_n^2}} e^{-\frac{(y_i-H)^2}{2\sigma_n^2}} \tag{5}$$

And the p.d.f of *H* is given by Eq. (6):

$$f(H) = \frac{1}{\sqrt{2\pi\sigma_H^2}} e^{-\frac{(H)^2}{2\sigma_H^2}} \tag{6}$$

It is known that the conditional p.d.f of H given y is in Eq. (7):

$$f(H|y) = \left\{ \frac{f(y|H)f(H)}{f(y)} \right\} \tag{7}$$

Inserting the values from Eqs. (5) and (6) in Eq. (7) provides Eq. (8):

$$f(H|y) = \left(\prod_{i=1}^{K} \frac{1}{\sqrt{2\pi\sigma_n{}^2}} \right) e^{-\sum_{i=1}^{K} \frac{1}{2\sigma_n{}^2}(y_i-H)^2} e^{-(H^2/2\sigma_H{}^2)} \frac{1}{f(y)\sqrt{2\pi}\sigma_H} \tag{8}$$

The expression in Eq. (8) can be defined in terms of q(y) as shown in Eq. (9):

$$f(H|y) = q(y)e^{-(1/2\sigma^2)\left(H-\sigma^2/\sigma_n{}^2\sum_{i=1}^{K}y_i\right)^2} \tag{9}$$

The notation σ is given by Eq. (10):

$$\sigma^2 = \frac{1}{(K\sigma_H{}^2 + \sigma_n{}^2)}\sigma_H{}^2\sigma_n{}^2 \tag{10}$$

It should be noted that q(y) is only the function of y; therefore, the best estimate H_{MAP} of H is the value where f(H|y) gets the highest peak, which is obtained from Eq. (11) when H = H_{MAP}:

$$H_{MAP} = \sigma^2/\sigma_n{}^2\sum_{i=1}^{K}y_i \tag{11}$$

Eq. (10) can be solved to get Eq. (12):

$$\sigma^2 = \frac{\sigma_H{}^2}{(\sigma_H{}^2 + \sigma_n{}^2/K)}\frac{1}{K}\sum_{i=1}^{K}y_i \tag{12}$$

If $\sigma_S{}^2 \gg \sigma_n{}^2/K$, then the best estimate of H is given as Eq. (13):

$$H_{MAP} \approx \frac{1}{K}\sum_{i=1}^{K}y_i \tag{13}$$

H_{MAP} is the best estimate of intensity levels of the character-containing region of a detected box, yet its value varies for every other detected box, and its probability distribution is also unknown, so it can also be assumed as a random variable that follows Gaussian distribution. If B represents the number of detected character boxes in a given image, then the set of real values $h_{MAP}(u)$ assigned to H_{MAP} for all detected boxes is shown in Eq. (14), where u represents the index of each box.

$$H_{MAP} = \{h_{MAP}(1), h_{MAP}(2), h_{MAP}(3), \ldots\ldots., h_{MAP}(\mathrm{B})\} \tag{14}$$

Let E [H_{MAP}] be the expectation of H_{MAP}, and it is expressed as Eq. (15). The variance σ 2H_{MAP} can be found in Eq. (16):

$$E\,[H_{MAP}] = \sum_{u=1}^{B} h_{MAP}(u)P\{H_{MAP} = h_{MAP}(u)\} \tag{15}$$

$$\sigma^2{}_{HMAP} = E\left[(H_{MAP} - E\,[H_{MAP}])^2\right] \tag{16}$$

Definition 1: (Set of bad boxes) The set of all those boxes such that members do not satisfy the conditions in Eq. (17) is called set of bad boxes.

Here n represents the quality index, and smaller value of n corresponds to higher demand of quality of label printing,

$$(E[H_{MAP}] - n\sigma_{HMAP}) \leq h_{MAP}(u) \leq (E[H_{MAP}] + n\sigma_{HMAP}) \tag{17}$$

The selection of bad box is performed by Eq. (17), as one of the main concerns in the quality inspection of label printing is to find the overly printed or faded printed characters. All the character boxes that fall under the stated condition Eq. (17) are considered as members of the set of good boxes. It is quite intuitive that high-quality printing demands larger set of good boxes. Therefore, the proposed scheme used two separated counters called GBc and BBc representing the numbers of good boxes and bad boxes, respectively. The % quality success for similar intensity levels QSI is given by Eq. (18):

$$QS_I = \frac{GB_c}{(BB_c + GB_c)} \times 100 \qquad (18)$$

It should also be noted that the value of QS_I has a direct relationship with quality index n. The smaller value of quality index means strict requirement of quality and for the same image QS_I decreases with the decrease in value of n and vice versa.

In order to plot the probability density estimate of H_{MAP}, the procedure for kernel density estimation [20] is used. It returns a probability density estimate f for the sampled data in the vector or two-column matrix. It estimates the density at 100 points for univariate data. **Figure 4** shows the plot of probability density estimate for H_{MAP} of the image in **Figure 3(a)**. It is clear that p.d.f approximately follows Gaussian curve with a certain value of mean and variances.

3.3.2 Detection of misprinted boxes

The detection of misprinted box is challenging in terms of its probability of occurrences and detection. The OCR engine can detect it as a text although being probably wrong detected and classified. The proposed scheme achieves the detection of misprinted box by deploying supervised machine learning using k-NN. The k-NN algorithm is a nonparametric method used for the classification and regression [21] in the pattern recognition. The supervised training aggregates the human responses to the appearance of a letter inside the detected box. The purpose of this step is to provide supervised learning samples and responses for the k-NN algorithm.

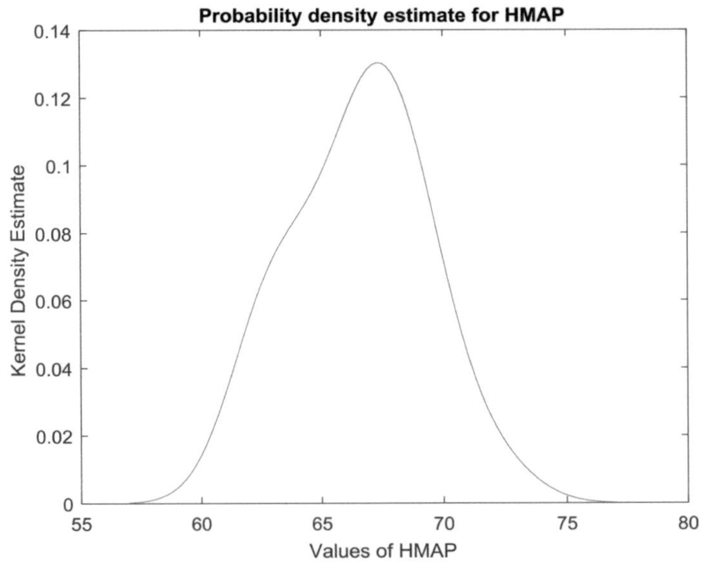

Figure 4.
*Kernel density estimate plot of H_{MAP} for the image in **Figure 3(a)**.*

The supervised machine learning procedure of the proposed scheme takes input sample image of industrial object which is printed with no defects. All the characters in this sample image are alphabets from A to Z, a to z, -, and numeric digits from 0 to 9. Let us call the set of these input images as no-misprinted-images (NMI). The training process starts by iterating the NMI for all detected boxes, and for each detected box, a human response is provided as a label and aggregated to a human responses database (HRD) file, because the human needs to press the related key from the keyboard. As for each detected letter box, its ratio width/height = 2/3; therefore each box is aggregated as a matrix of 20×30 pixels in separate matrices received database (MRD) file.

Therefore, at the end of training process, two (HRD and MRD) files are ready for the k-NN algorithm. The k-NN algorithm takes these two files as input and finds the nearest neighbor in terms of its output as hamming distance D as stated above. It is quite intuitive that D will have higher value for the misprinted or unknown letters, because the training process did not consider those letters. The value of D for each printed letter can be considered as a random variable sampled from a random process at time t, and since its distribution is also unknown, therefore, it is assumed that it follows Gaussian distribution. Based on the fact stated by [22], the proposed scheme also assumes that D is IID Gaussian random variable. The next step is finding the expectation of D for each letter box. It should be noted that D is normalized by the size of box, i. e., 20×30. Let us represent E[D] and σ_D^2 as the mean and variance of D. We can compute these values using the similar way as described in Eqs. (15) and (16), which provide the second order statistics for the distance. Let the set of real values d(u) assigned to the random variable D be given by Eq. (19):

$$D = \{d(1), d(2), d(3), \dots\dots, d(\mathrm{B})\} \tag{19}$$

Definition 2: (Misprinted box detection) The set of all those boxes such that members do not satisfy the conditions Eq. (20) is called set of misprinted bad boxes.

$$(E[D] - m\sigma_D) \leq d(u) \leq (E[D] + m\sigma_D) \tag{20}$$

Again the quality index m represents the strict boundary for the selection of misprinted boxes. All the character boxes that fall under the stated condition Eq. (20) are considered as members of the set of good printed boxes. It is quite intuitive that high-quality printing demands larger set of good boxes. Therefore, two separated counters called GPB_{count} and MPB_{count} represent the numbers of good printed boxes and misprinted boxes, respectively. The % quality success for good printed boxes QS_{GPB} is given by Eq. (21):

$$QS_{GPB} = \frac{GPB_{count}}{(MPB_{count} + GPB_{count})} \times 100 \tag{21}$$

The final step is the printing of the acquired results related to the text alignment, QS_I and QS_{GPB}. These results can not only draw the outcome of printing inspection process but can also provide feedback to the printing labelers to automatically adjust the process according to the type of printing errors.

4. Results

Table 1 summarizes the values of horizontal and vertical alignments for sample image in **Figure 5**. The results support the human observation of central text alignment for this kind of particular object. It should also be noted that text alignment specification and parameters are user specific.

Figure 6 shows the bar graph of the estimated values for the random variable H_{MAP} for each detected text in **Figure 3(b)**.

Figure 7 shows the histogram of H_{MAP} in terms of numbers of boxes and the value of random variable H_{MAP}. It also shows the corresponding normal distribution curve fitted based on the values of H_{MAP}.

Images	U	L	D	UD_{Thresh}	L_{Thresh}	Alignment testing	
						Horizontal	Vertical
1	42	59	50	170	119	Passed	Passed

Table 1.
Text alignment assessment results for the given image.

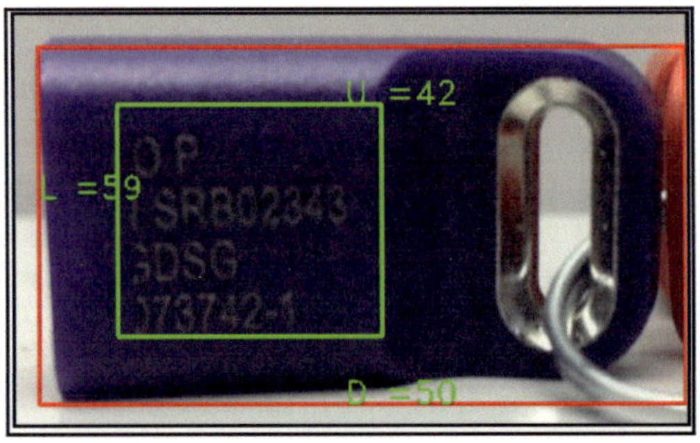

Figure 5.
Text alignment detection.

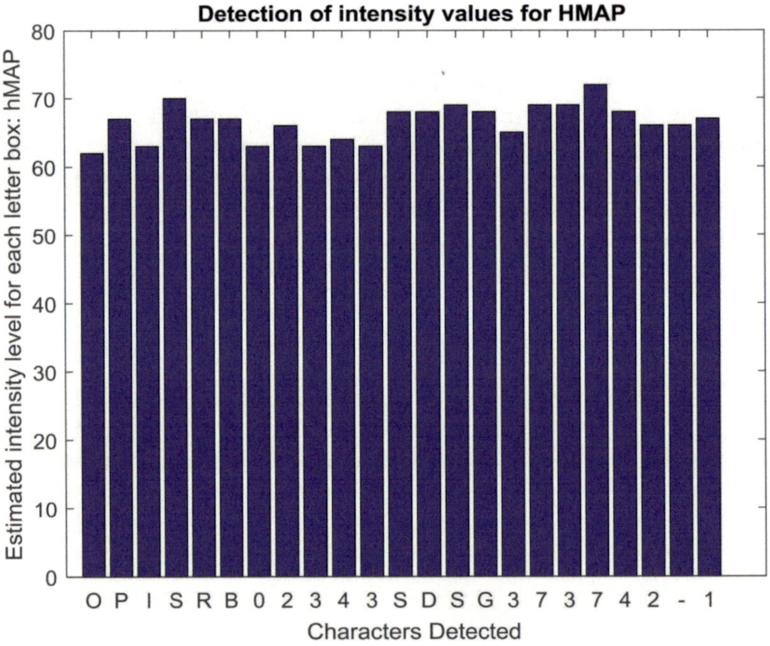

Figure 6.
Estimated intensity values of H_{MAP}.

Table 2 summarizes the results of printing quality assessment in order to test the intensity variations in the printed labels. It shows mean, variance, quality (Q) factor $n\sigma H_{MAP}$, the sum of good and bad boxes, and finally the QS_I. It is obvious from the results that Q factor decides the value of QS_I.

The value of quality index is varied as n = 1, 2, and 3 that increases the value of GBc as 13, 22, and 23, respectively. Additionally, the values for QS_I for n = 1, 2, and 3 are 56.52, 95.65, and 100%, respectively.

Figure 8 shows the output of SAML-QC scheme for the detection of bad printed labels. The higher quality control requires lower value of n.

Figure 8(a) shows that for the restriction n = 1, all good boxes are detected and marked with green color, whereas, all the boxes in red color are the ones with value of $h_{MAP}(u) \geq E[H_{MAP}] + n\sigma 2H_{MAP}$, whereas, boxes with $h_{MAP}(u) \leq E[H_{MAP}]$— $n\sigma 2H_{MAP}$ are represented by yellow boxes because they belong to the faded printing category. Similarly, **Figure 8(b)** and **(c)** shows the output images for n = 2 and 3, respectively.

The next assessment is related to the detection of misprinted characters, and **Figure 9** shows result of k-NN classification performed through supervised machine learning and the distance D for each detected character.

It is clear from the results in **Figure 9** that the two higher spikes for the detected character S and 3 are located at the position of misprinted characters.

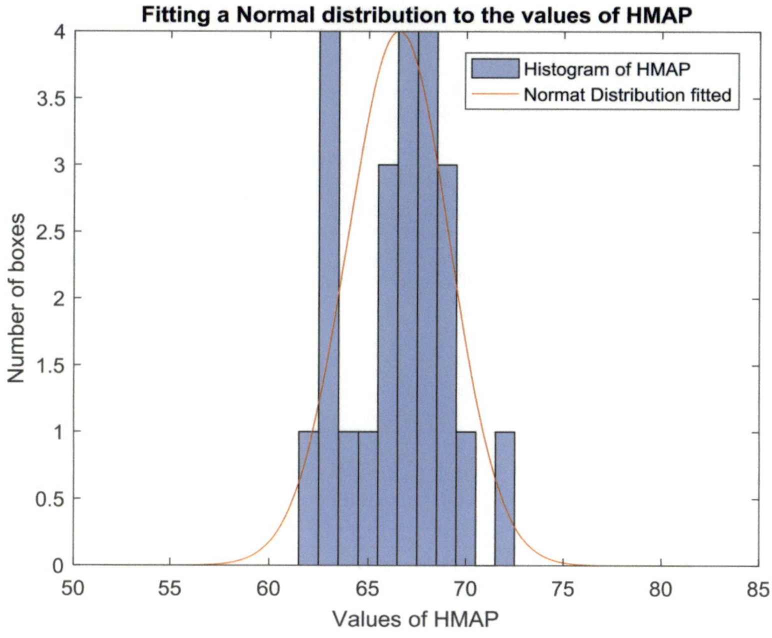

Figure 7.
Plot shows fitting a normal distribution to the values of H_{MAP}.

Q Index n	Mean E $[H_{MAP}]$	Variance σ $2H_{MAP}$	Q factor $n\sigma H_{MAP}$	Box counts GBc + BBc	QSI (%)
1	66	6	2.44	13 + 10	56.52
2	66	6	4.89	22 + 1	95.65
3	66	6	7.35	23 + 0	100

Table 2.
Printing quality assessment results for H_{MAP}.

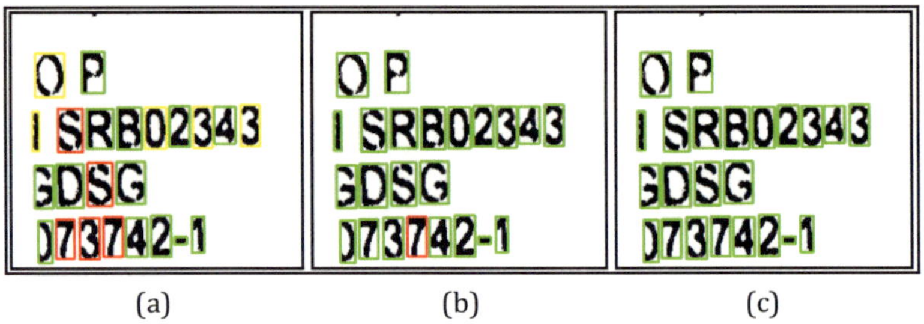

Figure 8.
Detection of bad printed boxes for different n: (a) n = 1, (b) n = 2, and (c) n = 3.

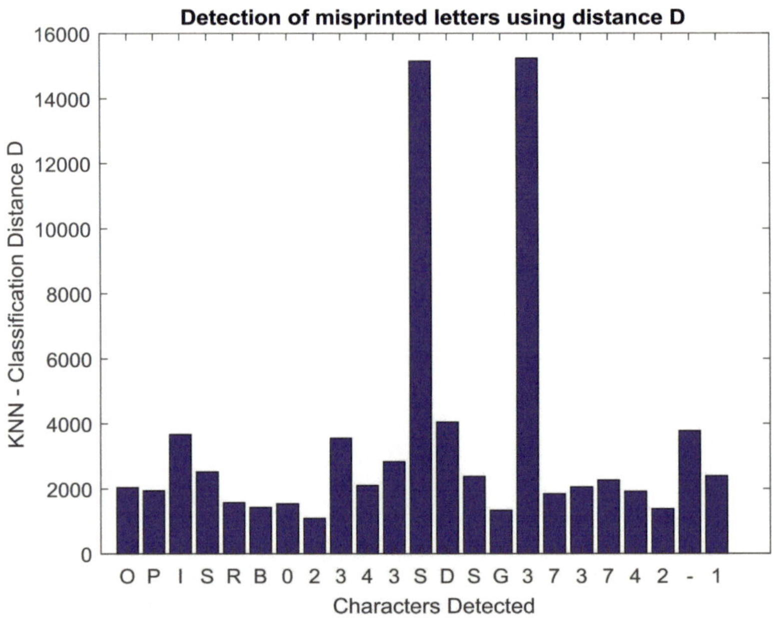

Figure 9.
Bar graph of k-NN classification distance D.

Quality index m	Mean E [D]	Variance σ_D^2	Q bound $n\sigma_D$	Box counts GPBc+MPBc	QSGBP %
1	3397.88	1.38 × 107	3727.68	21 + 2	91.30
2	3397.88	1.38 × 107	7455.36	21 + 2	91.30
3	3397.88	1.38 × 107	11183.04	21 + 2	91.30

Table 3.
Misprinted labels' assessment results.

Table 3 shows results of the process for the detection of misprinted boxes as discussed in Section 3. It is observed that the proposed scheme put a stable restriction on the misprinted labels, and it is shown in **Table 3** that the value of QSGBP remains 91.30% for all three values of m.

Figure 10 shows the detection of misprinted labels, and they are marked with the red boxes for m = 1, 2, and 3.

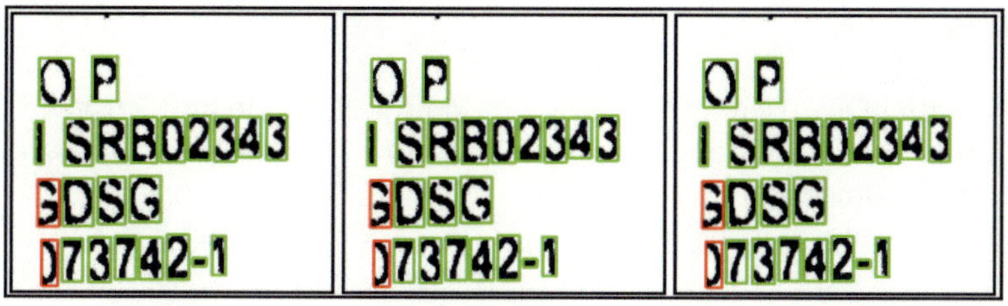

(a) (b) (c)

Figure 10.
Detection of misprinted boxes: (a) m = 1, (b) m = 2, and (c) m = 3.

5. Conclusions

This chapter proposes a stochastic assessment and machine vision-based technique to assess the printing quality of text on industrial objects. The assessment is based on three quality defects such as text misalignment, varying printing shades, and misprinted text. It is concluded from the results that second-order statistics related to the intensity values of pixels of text located under the threshold region of the original image can provide enough information to perform quality inspection. On the other hand, the hamming distance acquired by the k-NN supervised machine learning can also be taken as a random variable, and again the second-order statistics are helpful in order to detect the misprinted letter. In the future SAML-QC technique needs to be evaluated on various other images such as electronics parts and medical parts.

Acknowledgements

My deepest acknowledgment is to Prof. Tao JIANG of the College of Information and Communication Engineering, Harbin Engineering University, for guidance, kind support, and wisdom.

Author details

Azhar Hussain[1*] and Kamal Bhattarai[2]

1 Harbin Engineering University, Harbin, China

2 University of Engineering and Technology, Taxila, Pakistan

*Address all correspondence to: engrazr@gmail.com

References

[1] Label Printing Quality Management in China. 2018. Available from: http://narrowwebtech.com/narrowwebtech/label-printing-quality-management-in-china/

[2] Jurij R. The computer-aided detection of inferior printing quality and errors. In: Proceedings of IEEE MELECON; May 16–19; Benalmadena, Spain; 2006

[3] Huitno L. "A training-based no-reference image quality assessment algorithm." In: International Conference on image Processing (ICIP); 2004

[4] Rowley H et al. Neural network-based face detection. IEEE PAMI. 1998; **20**:22-38

[5] Viola P, Jones M. Rapid Object Detection Using a Boosted Cascade of Simple Features: In IEEE Conference on Computer Vision and Pattern Recognition. 2001

[6] Nahney I. Netlab: Algorithms for Pattern Recognition. Springer Verlag; 2001

[7] Islam MJ, Ahmadi M, Sid-Ahmed MA. Image processing techniques for quality inspection of gelatin capsules in pharmaceutical applications. In: 10th International Conference on Control, Automation, Robotics and Vision Hanoi, Vietnam; 17–20 December 2008

[8] Junfeng J, Xuejuan K, Pengfei L. Detection of the fabric printing quality based on the machine vision. In: International Conference on Intelligent Computation Technology and Automation; 2010

[9] Deng Y, Manjunath BS, Shin H. Color image segmentation. Processing of IEEE Computer Society Conference on Computer Vision and Pattern Recognition CVPR; 1999. pp. 451-466

[10] Li Xia AO, Xing Bin Z. Kind of image defect detection algorithm based on wavelet packet transform and blob analysis. In: Compute Center of Nanchang University; Nanchang, China

[11] Ritu B. Automated Quality Assessment of Printed Objects Using Subjective and Objective Methods Based on Imaging and Machine Learning Techniques; 2017

[12] Hines A, Kendrick P, Barri A, Narwaria M, Redi JA. Robustness and prediction accuracy of machine learning for objective visual quality assessment. 2014 22nd European Signal Processing Conference (EUSIPCO); Lisbon; 2014. pp. 2130-2134

[13] Gonzalez RC, Woods RE. Digital Image Processing. 3rd ed. ISBN 978-93-325-7032-0; 2008

[14] Jähne B, Scharr H, Körkel S. Principles of filter design. In: Handbook of Computer Vision and Applications. Academic Press; 1999

[15] Otsu N. A threshold selection method from gray-level histograms. IEEE Transactions on Systems, Man, and Cybernetics. 1979;**9**(1):62-66. DOI: 10.1109/TSMC.1979.4310076

[16] Tomasi C, Manduchi R. Bilateral filtering for gray and color images (PDF). Sixth International Conference on Computer Vision. Bombay; 1998. pp. 839-846. DOI: 10.1109/ICCV.1998.710815

[17] Kay A. Tesseract: An open-source optical character recognition engine. Linux Journal. 2007. Retrieved 28 September 2011

[18] Aaron C. A Brief Primer on Probability Distributions (PDF). Santa Fe Institute

[19] Hussain A, Shahzad K, Tang C. Real time speed estimation of vehicles. World Academy of Science, Engineering and Technology International Journal of Computer and Information Engineering. 2012;**6**(1):726-730

[20] Jones MC. Simple boundary correction for kernel density estimation. Statistics and Computing. 1998;**3**(3): 135-146

[21] Altman NS. An introduction to kernel and nearest-neighbor nonparametric regression. The American Statistician. 1992;**46**(3): 175-185

[22] Hippenstiel R, editor. Detection Theory: Applications and Digital Signal Processing. CRC Press; 2002

Chapter 8

Decision-Making in Real-Life Industrial Environment through Graph Theory Approach

Ravi Pratap Singh, Ravinder Kataria and Sandeep Singhal

Abstract

The approach called as "graph theory and matrix approach" has been well employed in numerous research studies with a view to perform the decision-making while the situation is becoming perplexed type or where there is a very strong relative importance of one parameter over another. In such cases, the said graph theory and matrix method provides very suitable and fruitful solutions to make the decision to its final effective extent. The further improvements and the outcome enhancement can also be revealed through the use of combined practice of graph theory results along with some artificial intelligence-inspired logics and practices such as fuzzy logic, artificial neural network, etc. The significance and applicability of said method in vast fields of science, engineering, and research are also proved. Nowadays, our manufacturing sectors are getting up to date through the applications of artificial intelligence and several software-based directions. This is all to enhance the overall machine system performance with a view to improve desired performance characteristics of the process under the study. Few sections of this chapter has also elaborated the utility of the artificial intelligence-inspired fuzzy logic-based decision system which has already been a part of previous researches.

Keywords: diagraph, computer systems, artificial intelligence, matrix, industries, fuzzy logic, artificial neural network

1. Basic overview of graph theory

The decision-making has now been developed and practiced with the use of several recently emerged methodologies to make the traditionally employed practices more effective and impressive [1–3]. The behavior of humans has been mimicked out in an effective and limited way through artificial intelligence models. Artificial neural networks, evolutionary computing, fuzzy logic, probabilistic analysis models, intelligent agents, etc. are some major tools which usually define the basic artificial intelligence system. Wren and Jain [4] have explored the application of artificial intelligence (AI) while practicing a healthy decision-making in practical industry-based problems. There are so many AI techniques which have been investigated in past researches for the purpose of decision-making [5, 6]. These methodologies are, namely, data trend analyzing, coordinating the data delivery, forecast providing, data consistency development, uncertainty quantification, etc. The well-known decision-making method, called *graph theory*, is a systematic and logical approach which also has proven to be useful for analyzing and modeling a wide range of applications in engineering and numerous other areas. This methodology is particularly based on the advanced theory of graphs, and therefore its applications are very well renowned. The demonstration through graph "or" digraph model has proven to be useful for modeling and analyzing numerous varieties of systems and problems in numerous fields of science and technology [7–9]. The approach based on the matrix method is useful in analyzing the graph/digraph models expeditiously to derive the system function and index to meet the objectives.

Graph theory is a subject of combinatorial mathematics and draws a lot from matrix theory. The matrix representation of the graph molds the problem to make use of computers for various complex operations. The graph theory and matrix methods (GTMM) consist of the digraph representation, the matrix representation, and the mathematical representation, i.e., a permanent function. The digraph is the visual representation of the variables and their interdependencies. The matrix converts the digraph into mathematical form, and the permanent function is a mathematical representation that helps to determine the numerical index [10, 11]. The graph theory approach is a systematic approach for conversion of qualitative factors to quantitative values, and mathematical modeling gives an edge to the proposed technique over conventional methods like cause-effect diagrams, flow charts, etc. These method outcomes can now be settled into some artificial intelligence-based tools and steps to generate some more fruitful and smart solutions. More specifically, the fuzzy logic-based approach can be implemented further to utilize the human thoughts regarding the problem under consideration. The logic generation will be based on the pure human experiences which help to implement the artificial intelligence-based graph theory approach more reasonable and practicable. The AI, generally described as the discipline of developing machines performing things that would entail human astuteness, is often perplexed with robotics, particularly humanoid robotics, as they are contiguous to "human" intellect. Graph theory has a wide range of applications in engineering and numerous other areas. The essential steps for executing the abovesaid methodology are as follows.

2. Selection of attributes

In this chief step, various characteristics which affect the outcome under study are identified, and the experimental design that gratifies the operation requirements is finalized. The trait values (T_i) and relative importance (u_{ij}) are obtained using **Tables 1** and 2.

2.1 Machinability attribute digraph representation

A digraph is exploited to illustrate the aspects which affect the machinability and interdependencies among them in terms of *edges* and *nodes*. A cluster of directed edges $R = \{u_{ij}\}$ and a cluster of nodes $Q = \{T_i\}$, with $i = 1, 2, \ldots, X$, consist in a digraph. A node *Ti* signifies the *i*th machinability attribute, and edges epitomize their relative importance. The number of nodes (X) reflected is the same as the number of machinability attributes considered for the machining operation. For example, three vital attributes, viz., material removal rate (1), tool wear rate (2), and surface roughness (3), are designated for the assessment of machinability work considered. The machinability characteristic diagraph is represented as shown in **Figure 1**.

S. no.	Qualitative measure of factors affecting machinability of titanium	Assigned value of machinability factors (T_i)
1.	Exceptionally low	0
2.	Extremely low	1
3.	Very low	2
4.	Below average	3
5.	Average	4
6.	Above average	5
7.	Moderate	6
8.	High	7
9.	Very high	8
10.	Extremely high	9
11.	Exceptionally high	10

Table 1.
Quantification of factors affecting machinability of titanium [12].

S. no.	Category description	Interdependencies of attributes	
		u_{ij}	$u_{ji} = 10\text{-}u_{ij}$
1.	Two attributes are of equal importance	5	5
2.	One attribute is slightly more important than the other	6	4
3.	One attribute is more important than the other	7	3
4.	One attribute is much more important than the other	8	2
5.	One attribute is extremely more important than the other	9	1
6.	One attribute is exceptionally more important than the other	10	0

Table 2.
Relative importance of machinability attributes (u_{ij}) [12].

2.2 Matrix representation of the machinability attribute digraph

The digraph is needed to be characterized in matrix form (H) called a variable permanent matrix for permanent machinability index (VPM_M). This is $X \times X$ matrix which deliberates all of the attributes (i.e., T_i) with their relative importance (i.e., u_{ij}). The matrix shown in Eq. (1) is articulated as per the machinability estimation digraph (**Figure 1**).

The tradition of the three imperative attributes is embodied by diagonal elements T1, T2, and T3, and interdependencies between them are revealed by off-diagonal elements of the matrix for individual attributes [12, 13].

For the deliberated machinability attribute digraph, the matrix H is illustrated as

$$VPM_M = H$$

$$= \begin{array}{c} \text{Attributes} \\ 1 \\ 2 \\ 3 \\ 4 \\ \cdots \\ \cdots \\ X \end{array} \begin{bmatrix} 1 & 2 & 3 & 4 & \cdots & \cdots & X \\ T_1 & u_{12} & u_{13} & u_{14} & \cdots & \cdots & u_{1X} \\ u_{21} & T_2 & u_{23} & u_{24} & \cdots & \cdots & u_{2X} \\ u_{31} & u_{32} & T_3 & u_{34} & \cdots & \cdots & u_{3X} \\ u_{41} & u_{42} & u_{43} & T_4 & \cdots & \cdots & u_{4X} \\ \cdots & \cdots & \cdots & \cdots & \cdots & \cdots & \cdots \\ \cdots & \cdots & \cdots & \cdots & \cdots & \cdots & \cdots \\ u_{X1} & u_{X2} & u_{X3} & u_{X4} & \cdots & \cdots & T_X \end{bmatrix} \quad (1)$$

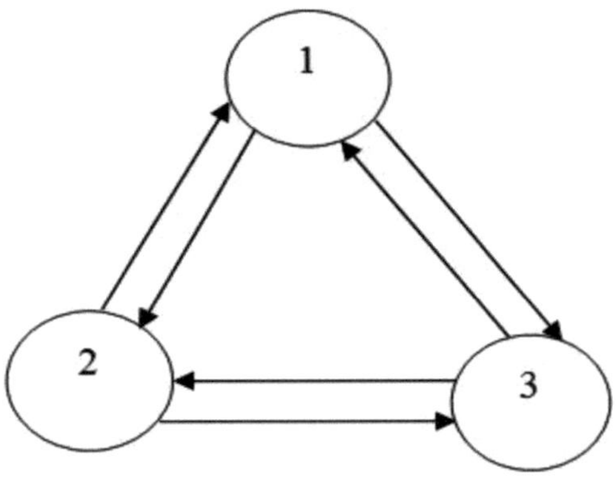

Figure 1.
Machinability attribute digraph representation.

Representation of this variable permanent matrix for VPM_M for the considered machinability attribute digraph (shown in **Figure 1**) is given below:

$$VPM_M = H$$

$$= \begin{array}{c} \text{Attributes} \\ \text{MRR} \\ \text{TWR} \\ \text{SR} \end{array} \begin{array}{c} \begin{array}{ccc} \text{MRR} & \text{TWR} & \text{SR} \end{array} \\ \begin{bmatrix} T_1 & u_{ij} & u_{ik} \\ u_{ji} & T_2 & u_{jk} \\ u_{ki} & u_{kj} & T_3 \end{bmatrix} \end{array} \tag{2}$$

2.3 Variable permanent function representation

The permanent of this matrix *H*, i.e., per (*H*), is distinct as the permanent machinability function. Machinability estimation signifies machinability traits of various experimental runs as measured. Furthermore, this tactic leads to avoid any loss of data as it does not carry any negative sign in the expression [12].

The "variable permanent machinability function" is expressed in sigma form as

$$\begin{aligned} \text{x per (H)} = {} & \prod_{i=1} T_i + \textstyle\sum_{i,j,\dots,X} (u_{ij}u_{ji})\, T_k T_l \dots T_X + \sum_{i,j,\dots X} (u_{ij}u_{jk}u_{ki} + u_{ik}u_{kj}u_{ji}) T_l T_m \dots T_X \\ & + \left\{ \textstyle\sum_{i,j,\dots X} (u_{ij}u_{ji})(u_{kl}u_{lk})\, T_m T_n \dots T_X + \displaystyle\sum_{i,j,\dots X} (u_{ij}u_{jk}u_{kl}u_{li} + u_{il}u_{lk}u_{kj}u_{ji})\, T_m T_n \dots T_X \right\} \\ & + \left[\textstyle\sum_{i,j,\dots X} (u_{lm}u_{ml})(u_{ij}u_{jk}u_{ki} + u_{ik}u_{kj}u_{ji}) T_n T_o \dots T_X + \sum_{i,j,\dots X} (u_{ij}u_{jk}u_{kl}u_{lm}u_{mi} + u_{im}u_{ml}u_{lk}u_{kj}u_{ji}) T_n T_o \dots T_X] \right] \\ & + [(\textstyle\sum_{i,j,\dots X} (u_{mn}u_{nm})(u_{ij}u_{jk}u_{kl}u_{li} + u_{il}u_{lk}u_{kj}u_{ji}) T_o \dots T_X + \sum_{i,j,\dots X} (u_{ij}u_{jk}u_{ki} + u_{ik}u_{kj}u_{ji})\, (u_{lm}u_{mn}u_{nl} + \\ & u_{ln}u_{nm}u_{ml})\, T_o \dots T_X + \textstyle\sum_{i,j,\dots X} (u_{ij}u_{ji})(u_{kl}u_{lk})(u_{mn}u_{nm})\, T_o \dots T_X \\ & + \textstyle\sum_{i,j,\dots X} (u_{ij}u_{jk}u_{kl}u_{lm}u_{mn}u_{ni} + u_{in}u_{nm}u_{ml}u_{lk}u_{kj}u_{ji})\, T_o \dots T_X) \end{aligned} \tag{3}$$

2.4 Evaluation of permanent machinability index

The permanent machinability function defined in Eq. (3) is engaged for appraisal of the permanent machinability index. The *permanent machinability index* is articulated as the arithmetical value of permanent machinability function.

All the assessable values of T_i are needed to be normalized on the similar scale as qualitative values, i.e., 0 to 10. For *beneficial machinability attributes*, the obligation of 0 and 10 is for smaller range value (T_{is}) and bigger range value (T_{ib}), respectively. Other midway values T_{ii} of the traits could also be dispensed in the scale from 0 to 10, as in Eq. (4):

$$\begin{aligned} T_i &= \{10/T_{ib}\} \times T_{ii} \quad \text{for } T_{is} = 0 \\ T_i &= \{10/(T_{ib} - T_{is})\} \times (T_{ii} - T_{is}) \quad \text{for } T_{is}>0 \end{aligned} \tag{4}$$

For *non-beneficial machinability attributes*, assignment of 0 and 10 is for bigger range value (T_{is}) and smaller range value (T_{ib}), respectively. Other intermediate values T_{ii} of the attributes could also be assigned in the scale from 0 to 10, as shown in Eq. (5):

$$\begin{aligned} T_i &= 10\{1 - (T_{ii}/T_{ib})\} \text{ for } T_{is} = 0 \\ T_i &= \{10/(T_{ib} - T_{is})\} \times (T_{ib} - T_{ii}) \text{ for } T_{is}>0 \end{aligned} \tag{5}$$

Relative interdependency amid two traits (i.e., u_{ij}) for the considered project is also allotted as a value over the range from 0 to 10 and is arranged into six categories. The interdependency between two attributes can be distributed on the scale 0 to 10 as given below:

$$u_{ij} = 10 - u_{ji} \tag{6}$$

The investigational runs are then arranged in down/rising order as per the calculated values of permanent machinability index. The investigational run having the *highest value* of permanent machinability index is chosen as the *best alternative* for the task under deliberation.

2.5 Identification and comparison of different available alternatives

Let V_{ij} signify the total assessment of the terms of *j*th sub-clustering of the *i*th clustering of the variable permanent machinability function. For the case of no sub-grouping, then the situation will be $V_{ij} = V_i$, i.e., total assessment of terms of the *i*th clustering. The identification set for an experimental run for the considered machining process is

$$/V_1/V_2/V_3/V_4/V_{51} + V_{52}/V_{61} + V_{62}/ \tag{7}$$

A contrast between any two investigational runs can also be made by using Eq. (8). On the basis of divergence of performance, the dissimilarity coefficient (C_d) for any two investigational runs is proposed as

$$C_d = (1/B)\sum\Phi_{ij}, \text{i, j} \tag{8}$$

where B = max. of [$\sum |V_{ij}|$ and $\sum |V'_{ij}|$], i,j i,j

The assessments of the terms for the variable permanent machinability function (V_{ij} and V'_{ij}) for two investigational run under the estimation and contrast, and $\Phi_{ij} = |V_{ij} - V'_{ij}|$. The similarity coefficient is also expressed as

$$C_s = 1 - C_d \tag{9}$$

2.6 Coefficients of similarity and dissimilarity

The calculation is being performed for similarity and dissimilarity coefficients as per Eqs. (8) and (9).

3. Case studies on graph theory: a view on real-life problem solving

There are so many investigations that have been carried out by the numerous researchers throughout the globe in the domain of graph theory and its allied approaches to study and analyze the method's applicability and reliability. The further optimization of the process under the study can also help the investigator to attain better and effective research outcomes [1, 14]. The discussion has also been explored by incorporating the possibilities to use the artificial intelligence-inspired logics in collaboration with the established graph theory approach. In this way, some case studies are reviewed and presented below to provide an overview which can explore about the major findings of the researches persuaded and the state-of-the-art representation of past investigations in the best conclusive manner. The selected case studies are as follows.

3.1 Machinability evaluation of work materials

Rao and Gandhi [8, 9] have presented a graph theory-based methodology with a view to evaluate the machinability of work materials for a given machining operation. They have proposed a universal machinability index that evaluates and ranks work materials for a given machining operation. The development of a digraph was also conducted to reflect the machinability attributes and their relative importance for the operation considered. The coefficients of similarity and dissimilarity and the identification sets have also been proposed. Disparate the traditional methods which adopt only one of the machinability assessment criteria, their proposed method has considered all of the criteria simultaneously and gives the correct and complete evaluation of the machinability of work materials. They have concluded that their proposed universal machinability index evaluates and ranks work materials for the considered machining operation. When it comes to taking the combined advantages of the features of artificial intelligence with the graph theory approach, the process moderation always becomes more crucial to consider. The requirements of the end customer regarding the produced goods further become extensively vital.

3.2 Selection of industrial robot

Rao and Padmanabhan [15] have conducted a research study based on graph theory method for the evaluation of alternative industrial robots. They have attained a robot selection index that evaluates and ranks robots for a considered industrial application. The calculated index was obtained from a robot selection attribute function, obtained from the robot selection attribute digraph. They have reported that the obtained similarity index from robot selection attribute function which was quite useful for easy storage and retrieval of the data. The proposed study was a general methodology, and there can be any number of quantitative and qualitative robot selection attributes simultaneously and offers a more objective, simple, and consistent robot selection approach. Their proposed robot selection index has been utilized to evaluate and rank the robots for the selected robot selection problem. In addition, the expectation of the end user of the robotic system can also be provided perfectly by properly understanding and practicing the modeling and simulation methodologies related to the artificial intelligence. Furthermore, the decision support system also helps to gather, analyze, and trend forming of the existing demands of the customer or end product user [16, 17].

3.3 Failure cause analysis of machine tools

Rao and Gandhi [8, 9] have analyzed the failure reasons of a machine tool by means of digraph and matrix approaches. The machine tool failure causation digraph has been modeled a failure reason taking into deliberation its failure-backing actions and their contact in terms of the reason—consequence relationship. After that, they have determined machine tool failure causation function from the machine tool failure causation matrix. The said matrix was attained through the digraph, which is distinctive of the failure root. The obtained function was not only convenient for failure reason analysis but likewise for comparison and appraisal of the failure reason. In addition, the machine tool failure causality index, derived from the machine tool failure causality function, had also been proposed, which evaluated and ranked the failure causes of a machine tool.

The attained machine tool failure causation function has identified the backing failure occasions of a machine tool that were decisive for minimization of the failure root and also supports in contrast and assessment of the failure source of a machine tool. The arithmetical value of the machine tool failure causation function has also been computed and named as *the machine tool failure cause index*. This index has been concluded as a measure of the severity of the failure cause. Furthermore, an artificial intelligence-inspired fuzzy logic-based system can properly help to make the problem more realistic, and the causes of the tool failures can be resolved out or eliminated [18, 19]. The AI-based process optimization is another domain where the failure reduction and the overall performance improvement can be settled out.

3.4 Selection of rapid prototyping process

Rao and Padmanabhan [20] have employed a graph theory-based methodology for selection of a rapid prototyping (RP) process that best suits the end use of a given product or part. The "rapid prototyping process selection index" has been also anticipated to estimate and rank the RP progressions for constructing a given product. The index was gained from an RP procedure assortment attribute function, acquired from the RP course selection attribute digraph. The digraph is established considering RP method assortment attributes and their relative importance for the deliberated application. The projected process reflects RP process variety attributes and their interrelations, and the RP process assortment index evaluates and ranks RP processes for a given RP procedure collection problem. The projected method was observed as a broad technique and capable to deliberate any number of measurable and qualitative RP course assortment attributes concurrently and proposes a more objective and modest RP method selection approach.

3.5 Performance evaluation of carbide compacting die

Jangra et al. [21, 22] conducted a study to assess the concert of carbide compacting die by means of graph theory approach (GTA). Factors influencing the die performance and their relations were analyzed by evolving a mathematical model by employing the digraph-based matrix method. The die performance index was attained through the matrix model established from the developed digraphs. This index value has compared and ranked the factors distressing the die performance. They have considered several process output errors such as dimensional inaccuracy, large surface craters, deep recast layers, etc. that have been minimized during die manufacturing which further helps to achieve better die performance. They have formed a group of factors upsetting the presentation of carbide compacting die into major five factors, viz., machine tool, work material, the geometry of die, tool electrode, and processing operation. The GTA procedure revealed that the machine tool had the maximum value of the index. Consequently, they have considered it as the utmost persuading factor influencing the die performance. Furthermore, they have also reported that in the event of die material, low cobalt concentration and lesser grain size harvest decent surface finish, while in machine tool, low discharge energy and high dielectric flow rate yield good surface finish. In the case of die geometry, large workpiece thickness and small taper angles result in lesser geometrical deviations.

Through this methodology, they have quantified the weak and strong factors which help in efficient process planning during die manufacturing, consequently. The GTA practice revealed that the machine tool had an uppermost value of the computed index. Therefore, it was considered as the most influencing parameter affecting the die performance.

While in respect of the die material, small grain size and low cobalt concentration yielded decent surface finish; however, in the case of the machine tool, low discharge energy and high dielectric flow rate yielded good surface finish and hence favors the good die performance. In the case of die geometry, large workpiece thickness and small taper angles reported in slighter geometrical deviances hence aid to attain better die performance. Die performance was articulated in terms of an index. This index value was depending on the inheritance of main factors which was further depending on their sub-factors. Therefore, a suitable combination of the sub-system and their sub-factors could easily be selected for the required die performance.

Singh et al. [23] have reported the optimization of the process inputs while processing composite material using ultrasonic machining using fuzzy logic-based smart decision- and rule making. The overall fuzzy system possesses the basic elements particularly fuzzy sets, fuzzy rulings, fuzzy inference, membership functions, and defuzzification [24–26]. The basic fuzzy logic system is illustrated in **Figure 2**. They have also explored the utility of the fuzzy logic-based ruling for the proper implementation of the human neural system logics. **Figure 3** is describing the employed triangular membership functions for the composite problem [23].

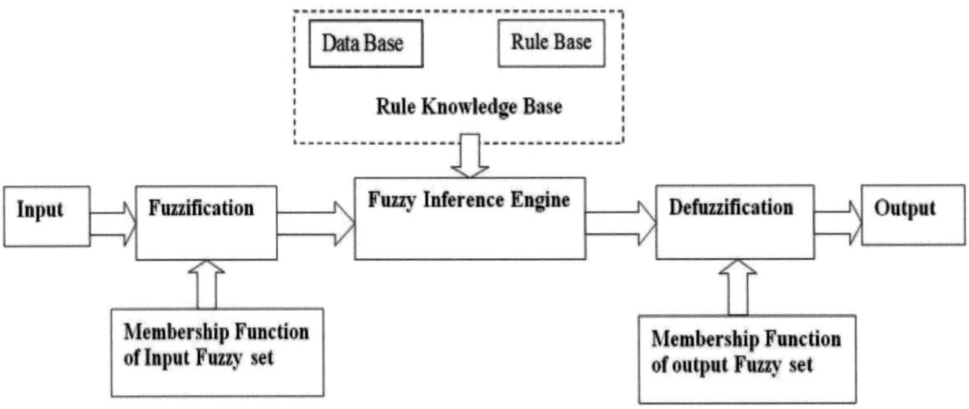

Figure 2.
The fuzzy logic system.

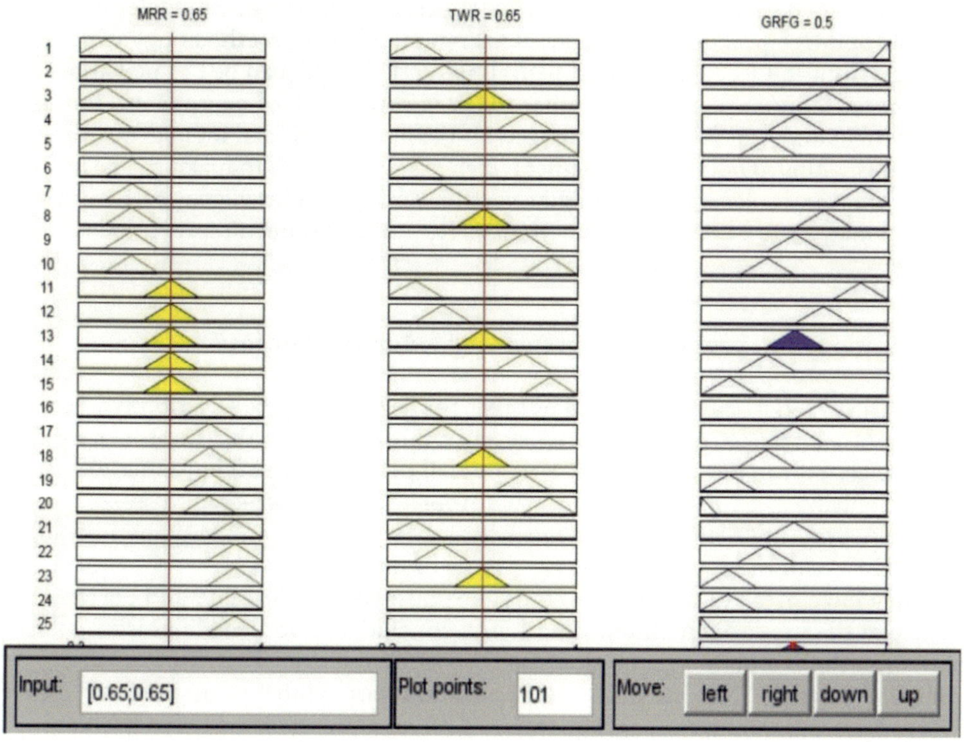

Figure 3.
Triangular membership functions of fuzzy system.

3.6 Analysis and evaluation of product design

Paramasivam and Senthil [1] have explored that the product design evaluation is essential for all manufacturing industries to explore the soundness and effectiveness of the product design. In their study, they presented a mathematical model for evaluating and analyzing the product design alternatives using graph theory and matrix approach. The different contributing factors were identified, and their relative importance was considered. A digraph model was constructed to represent the abstract information of the product design which takes into account all the factors. The digraph model was then transformed into a matrix form, which further was employed for computer processing. A permanent index was attained from the product design appraisal function, consequent from the matrix for all product design substitutes, and it showed the effectiveness of the product design. The indices were also deliberated for all the alternatives under study, and they were graded in rising order, and the product design analogous to the first rank was selected as the finest one.

Their proposed practice was quite adaptable from the opinion that it incorporates all factors of the product design. The GTM method was explored as pertinent to any product design entailing of any number of variables. The utility of matrix algebra was found to be expedient both for pictorial and computer analysis. The product design assessment index has represented the product design features and was useful in positioning the several product models based on the design facets. It was also concluded that the GTM method can be applicable to various problems of incompatible nature and to the problems, where the measurable data are not obtainable, i.e., machine cell layout analysis, material handling system evaluation, vehicle routing optimization, supplier selection problem, etc. Furthermore, the results obtained through the graph theory approach can easily be modeled through the collaborative practice through artificial neural network methodology which is inspired from the AI. The artificial neural network (ANN) can be defined as an interconnected group of nodes, similar to the vast network of neurons in a human brain. Duan and Yeh [27] have practiced and explored artificial intelligence-based decision-making. They have implemented the said approach to make the decision for accounting choice evaluation and selection through an intelligent system-based methodology. The basic illustration of an ANN model has been represented in **Figure 4**.

3.7 Selection of appropriate equipment for industrial purpose

Safari et al. [28] have explained out that proper equipment selection is a very important activity for manufacturing systems due to the fact that improper equipment selection can negatively affect the overall performance and productivity of a manufacturing system. They have further implemented a two-step fuzzy-analytical hierarchy process (AHP) and graph theory matrix approach (GTMA) methodology, i.e., GTMA uses fuzzy-AHP result weights as input weights.

They have presented a real-life study to reflect the applicability and performance of the proposed methodology. It was concluded that using linguistic variables, the evaluation process can become more realistic. The usage of fuzzy-AHP weights in GTMA has made the application more realistic and reliable. The proposed model was only implemented on an equipment selection problem in the company. They have further suggested the possibilities to employ other

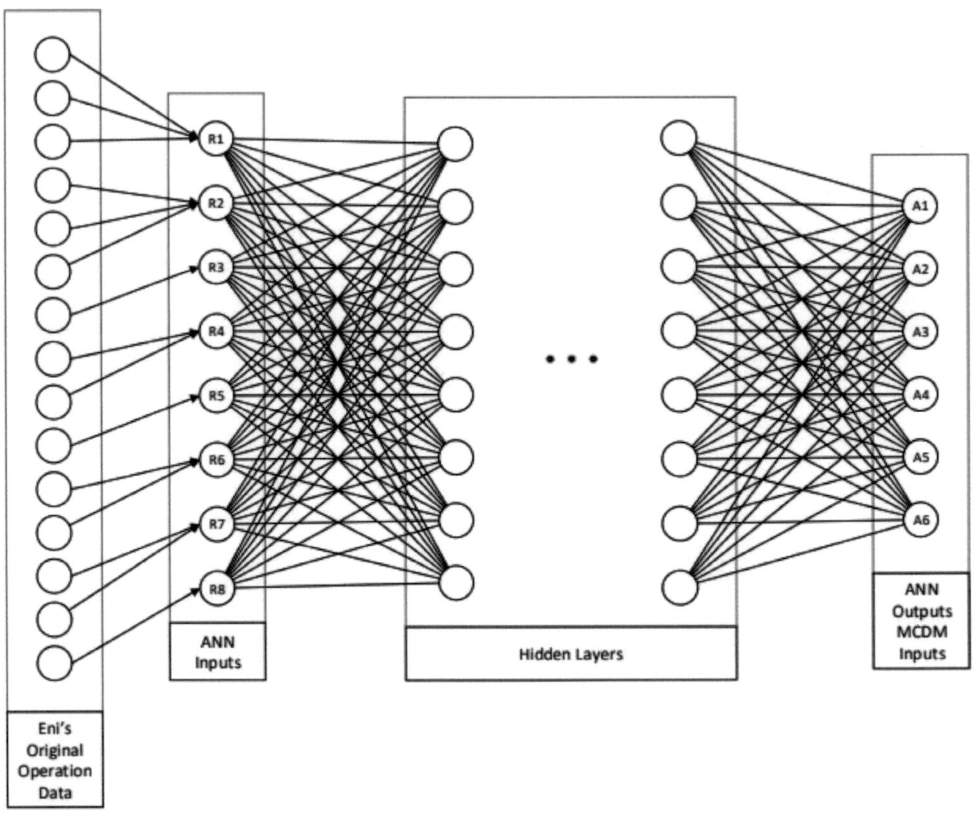

Figure 4.
Illustration of an artificial neural network (ANN) model.

decision-making methods such as fuzzy ELECTRE, fuzzy GTMA, and interval GTMA as a future direction.

3.8 Machinability study of commercial pure titanium

Singh et al. [10] have utilized the graph theory-based matrix method for the study of machinability of commercially pure titanium. In general, the single and multiple response optimization of any machining processes gives a different shape to the problem to elaborate it in the most better way and further makes the system more reliable and productive [29, 30]. They further said that any type of processing method is well subjective by the machinability of the work material under study. They have proposed a GTMM-based practice for the valuation of machinability of titanium workpiece in ultrasonic drilling.

Identification of numerous process attributes along with their relative prominence was undertaken and analyzed by mounting a mathematical function by engaging GTMM. Furthermore, an attribute digraph was also established, which has provided them with a visual image of reflected attributes with their relative connections. The developed digraph was further embodied by using matrix relation. A permanent machinability index for all the investigational runs was also attained from matrix form demonstration built on attribute digraph. The blend of all the attributes for any processing approach has made the proposed method quite versatile. The results have revealed that an experimental run having the combination consisting tool material of titanium, grit size of 500, and a power supply of 300 W yielded optimized results for machinability.

4. Conclusions

The application and the capability of artificial intelligence-inspired fuzzy logic-based decision-making have been discussed. The graph theory-based decision-making method has also been explored to employ in practical industrial situations. The following major inferences can be drawn from the proposed chapter. These are:

- The discussed methodology, namely, graph theory, is capable enough to handle the versatile real-life situation as this method includes the several input factors and their sub-factors too.

- The graph theory and matrix methods consist of the digraph representation, the matrix representation, and the mathematical representation, i.e., a permanent function. The digraph is the visual representation of the variables and their interdependencies.

- From the domain of AI, there are some observed major practices, namely, artificial neural networks, evolutionary computing, fuzzy logic, probabilistic analysis models, intelligent agents, etc., which usually define the basic artificial intelligence system.

- The artificial intelligence-inspired logics and practices can make the traditional decision-making more effective and versatile too. The fuzzy logic-based decision-making has emerged as one of the basic collaborative exercise conducted to offer viable solutions to any domain of real-life practical problems. The computation involved in these methods is simple, effective, and moreover quite friendly for the decision-makers.

- The triangular and the trapezoidal membership function of a fuzzy-based logic can also offer the conceptual-based rule making and decision-making.
- The demonstrated case studies from the different past researches explored about the applicability of the suggested method in numerous industries ranging from the manufacturing, service industries, robotic industries, die-making firms, automobiles, etc.

Conflict of interest

There is no conflict of interest.

Author details

Ravi Pratap Singh[1*], Ravinder Kataria[2] and Sandeep Singhal[3]

1 Department of Industrial and Production Engineering, Dr. B.R. Ambedkar National Institute of Technology, Jalandhar, Punjab, India

2 School of Mechanical Engineering, LPU, Jalandhar, Punjab, India

3 Department of Mechanical Engineering, NIT, Kurukshetra, Haryana, India

*Address all correspondence to: ravipratap.1512@gmail.com; singhrp@nitj.ac.in

References

[1] Singh RP, Singhal S. Rotary ultrasonic machining: A review. Materials and Manufacturing Processes. 2016;**31**:1795-1824

[2] Pomerol JC. Artificial intelligence and human decision making. European Journal of Operational Research. 1996; **99**:3-25

[3] Hertz L, Krogh A, Palmer RG. Introduction to the Theory of Neural Computing. Addison Wesley; 1991

[4] Wren GP, Jain L. Artificial intelligence for decision making. Springer Publications. 2006;**LNCS-4252**:531-536

[5] Fodor J, Roubens M. Fuzzy Preference Modelling and Multicriteria Decision Support. Kluwer; 1994

[6] Nowicki R, Slowinski R, Stefanowski J. Evaluation of vibroacoustic diagnostic symptoms by means of the rough sets theory. Computers in Industry. 1992;**20**: 141-152

[7] Singh RP, Singhal S. Experimental investigation of machining characteristics in rotary ultrasonic machining of quartz ceramic. Proceedings of the Institution of Mechanical Engineers, Part L: Journal of Materials Design and Applications. 2016;**232**:870-889

[8] Rao RV, Gandhi OP. Digraph and matrix methods for the machinability evaluation of work materials. International Journal of Machine Tools & Manufacture. 2002;**42**:321-330

[9] Rao RV, Gandhi OP. Failure cause analysis of machine tools using digraph and matrix methods. International Journal of Machine Tools & Manufacture. 2002;**42**:521-528

[10] Singh RP, Kumar J, Kataria R, Singhal S. Investigation of the machinability of commercially pure titanium in ultrasonic machining using graph theory and matrix method. Journal of Engineering Research. 2015;**3**: 75-94

[11] Singh RP, Singhal S. Rotary ultrasonic machining of macor ceramic: An experimental investigation and microstructure analysis. Materials and Manufacturing Processes. 2016;**32**: 927-939

[12] Rao RV. Decision Making in Manufacturing Environment. Springer Publications; 2007

[13] Paramasivam V, Senthil V. Analysis and evaluation of product design through design aspects using digraph and matrix approach. International Journal on Interactive Design and Manufacturing. 2009;**3**:13-23

[14] Singh RP, Singhal S. Investigation of machining characteristics in rotary ultrasonic machining of alumina ceramic. Materials and Manufacturing Processes. 2016;**32**:309-326

[15] Rao RV, Padmanabhan KK. Selection, identification and comparison of industrial robots using digraph and matrix methods. Robotics and Computer-Integrated Manufacturing. 2006;**22**:373-383

[16] Pomerol JC, Roy B, Sabroux CR, Saad A. An intelligent DSS for the multicriteria evaluation of railway timetables. Foundations of Computer and Decision Science. 1995;**20**:219-238

[17] Rasmussen J. Skills, rules and knowledge, signals, signs and symbols and other distinctions in human performance models. IEEE Transactions SMC. 1983;**13**:257-266

[18] Dubois D, Prade H. Fuzzy Sets and Systems: Theory and Applications. Academic Press; 1980

[19] Rasmussen J. The Human as a System Component—Human Interaction with Computer. Academic Press; 1980

[20] Rao RV, Padmanabhan KK. Rapid prototyping process selection using graph theory and matrix approach. Journal of Materials Processing Technology. 2007;**194**:81-88

[21] Jangra K, Grover S, Chan FTS, Aggrawal A. Digraph and matrix method to evaluate the machinability of tungsten carbide composite with wire EDM. International Journal of Advanced Manufacturing Technology. 2011;**56**: 959-974

[22] Jangra K, Grover S, Aggrawal A. Digraph and matrix method for the performance evaluation of carbide compacting die manufactured by wire EDM. International Journal of Advanced Manufacturing Technology. 2011;**54**: 579-591

[23] Singh RP, Kataria R, Kumar J, Verma J. Multi-response optimization of machining characteristics in ultrasonic machining of WC-Co composite through Taguchi method and grey fuzzy logic. AIMS Material Science. 2018;**5**: 75-92

[24] Newell A. The knowledge level. Artificial Intelligence. 1982;**18**:87-127

[25] Nilsson JJ. Principles of Artificial Intelligence. TIOGA Publishing Company; 1980

[26] Zadeh LA. Fuzzy sets as a basis for a theory of possibility. Fuzzy Sets and Systems. 1978;**1**:3-28

[27] Duan Y, Yeh CH. An intelligent system based approach to accounting choices evaluation and selection. In: Proceedings of Pacific Asia Conference on Information Systems (PACIS). 2018

[28] Safari H, Faghih A, Fathi MR. Integration of graph theory and matrix approach with fuzzy AHP for equipment selection. Journal of Industrial Engineering and Management. 2013;**6**:477-494

[29] Singh RP, Singhal S. Experimental study on rotary ultrasonic machining of alumina ceramic: Microstructure analysis and multi-response optimization. Proceedings of the Institution of Mechanical Engineers, Part L: Journal of Materials Design and Applications. 2016. DOI: 10.1177/1464420716657370

[30] Singh RP, Singhal S. An experimental study on rotary ultrasonic machining of macor ceramic. Proceedings of the Institution of Mechanical Engineers, Part B: Journal of Engineering Manufacture doi. 2016. DOI: 10.1177/0954405416666897